THOROUGHBREDS

THOROUGH

MORNING ON THE MOHAWK
NATURE'S OWN HIGHWAY, THE WATER LEVEL ROUTE
The Twentieth Century Limited
of the NEW YORK CENTRAL LINES

BREDS

NEW YORK CENTRAL'S

4-6-4 HUDSON

THE MOST FAMOUS CLASS

OF STEAM LOCOMOTIVE

IN THE WORLD

THOROUGHBREDS

by Alvin F. Staufer

research by Edward L. May

edited and published by Alvin F. Staufer

Library of Congress Catalog Card No. 74-75354

printed in the United States

ISBN 0-944513-03-4

First Printing 1975
Second Printing 1986
Third Printing 1998

© 1974 by Alvin F. Staufer. All rights reserved. This book may not be reproduced in part or in whole without written permission from the publisher. Published by Alvin F. Staufer, 3186 Stony Hill Rd., Medina, Ohio 44256.

Al Staufer collection

1939 poster of 20th Century Limited.

ACKNOWLEDGEMENTS

My total experience (2 months section hand timekeeper and 3 months bulk mail handler) puts me as close to the realities of railroading as Sociology professors are to the realities to poverty and the everyday work ethic. This view from the summit, while somewhat desireable, is insufficient to probe the dirt and grease of motive power realities, so I am more than most dependent on others.

From the New York Central there was Ann Kuss and Ed Nowak. Photographic help from fans is vital. So vital that without them, this book could not be. In part there were: Norton D. (Skip) Clark, Al Johnson, Bob Buck, R. Ganger, Dick Jacobs, Wilson Jones, Paul Prescott, H. Stirton, W. Rossiter, Bob Lorenz, Jim Seacrest, Si Herring, R. Whitbeck, Bert Pennypacker, H. K. Vollrath, Roger Rasor and Vance Roth.

Since I work totally alone, there is a dependence on friends who help contribute the abstracts — or "why's". Primarily, they are Don Speidel, Keith Buchanan, Cal Banse and Jack McGroarty.

The craftsman from Staufer Litho Plate did wonders with graphic reproductions, particularly the old posters.

The indispensible man was Ed May. His life-long love and pursuit of New York Central is recorded in this volume, both in pictures and words. He did much of the engine research and everything, to do with passenger cars and trains.

To these and the many others whose contributions are slightly less visable, I am most grateful.

Sincerely,

Al Staufer

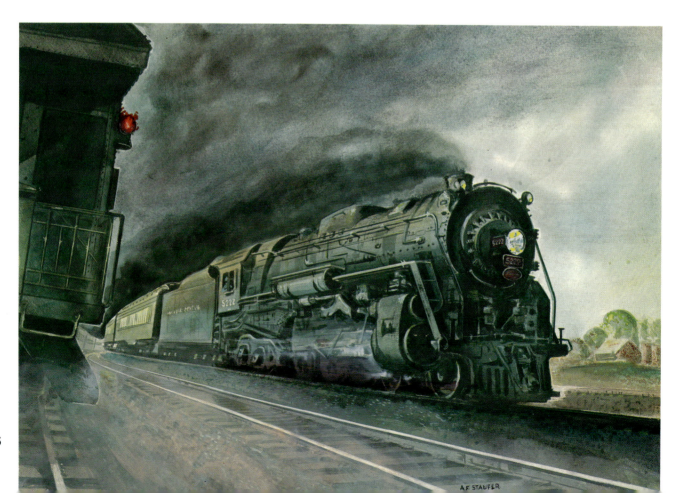

CONTENTS

What Came Before	14
The First Hudson	38
The J1 Fleet	66
J2's for the B&A	130
J3 Super Hudsons	156
Streamlining	202
The Most Famous Hudson	230
Wrecks	246
The Great Steel Fleet	256
From the Men	290
What Followed	304
Other Hudsons	312
Toys and Models	320
Art and Plans	332

Empire State Express poster by Leslie Ragan.

New York Central

INTRODUCTION

When we write about the New York Central Hudson we write about a different America. In 1927 the country was experiencing a post war boom. The tempo of business and travel was accelerated at an artificial rate, fueled by a national optimism that knew no bounds.

These were days before federal and municipal governments were stumbling over each other building airports and freeways. These were the days of rail dominance of the transportation scene. New York City based Central was caught in the crush. They were the most famous, even though second in size to the gigantic Pennsylvania. If you were Anyone heading west, odds are you would almost automatically select the "Century".

The locomotive developed by the princely New York Central to meet these ever increasing demands was the 4-6-4 Hudson type. There, in great part lies her fame. She was **the locomotive for the road** at the height of rail passenger travel in America.

That she was the first of her wheel arrangement in the United States matters not nearly as much as what she hauled and how she hauled it. The Hudson was designed to haul the "Great Steel Fleet" on the "Water Level Route". They were a New York Central phenomenon. They were a special machine for that special road. That in essence is what made them the most famous class of steam locomotive in the world.

But there was more to the legend then simply "doing the job". They looked the part. So how do we objectively evaluate the aesthetics of 200 tons of living iron? Generally, the old "beauty is in the eye of the beholder" bit contains a regional "truth", but it is nontheless conceded by most that New York Central's Hudson is one of, if not the most beautiful of all steam locomotives. Why? Well first there is the luck of having all the necessary parts just looking good. Then there are the physical limitations imposed by the railroad itself. On the New York Central it was simply low clearances. This dictated a "straight through" look that not only affected the Hudson but all of Central's power during the Golden Years. Working within these limitations, the designers of both American Locomotive Co. and New York Central created the final product.

The Hudsons had it all; looks, performance and timing. And as we shall see, fame is a self perpetuating thing. They were synonymous with the best. They were the best.

This is their story.

Alvin F. Staufer

Vermilion, Ohio - 1972

Hudsons at Harmon, New York.   Al Staufer collection

5344, the most famous Hudson of all, drifts into a station stop somewhere in up-state New York.
24x30" oil by Craig Staufer

CLEVELAND UNION TERMINAL

Picture postcard of 1918 proclaiming Cleveland's new lakefront terminal - except it was never built.

1927

1927 was a vintage year in transportation. The most notable event was the introduction of Ford's Model "A". Unknown to most it was also the year of the Hudson locomotive.

Sid Davis - Glenn Monhart collection

Famous racing plane and pilot, Art Chester, poses beside his Menasco powered "Jeep" with Ford Trimotor in background about 1931.

American Air Racing Society

American Air Racing Society

Model "A" Ford and Curtiss Robin.
Why do we like these things so much? Is it because we were simply raised with them or is there an intrinsic charm in this very functional not quite streamlined design.

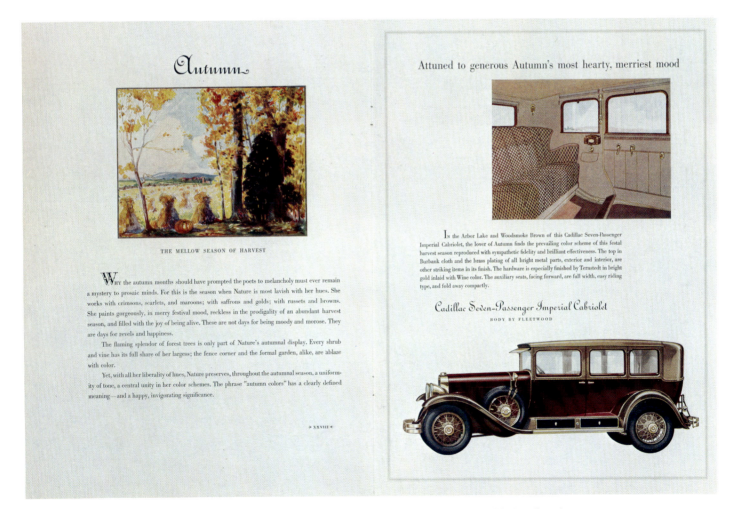

In 1927, Cadillac introduced its 28 line with a fabulous booklet titled "Color Creations from Nature's Studios". The theme on these two pages is "Autumn".
Reproduced here through the courtesy of Cadillac Division, General Motors Corporation.

WHAT CAME

BEFORE

Norton D. Clark

THE ROAD

In the beginning was the land. We emphasize the point because in most evaluations of steam locomotives nothing of such importance is discussed in the least.

The route of the New York Central is the finest in the Eastern United States. This trail is the only break in the great mountain chain that extends up and down the continent from New England to Alabama. From New York City the road hugs the east bank of the Hudson River for about 150 miles to Albany. Between Albany and Schenectady the rise is 200 ft. while the very highest point between New York City and the Great Lakes is 888 ft. at Batavia. From Buffalo to Chicago the road (old Lake Shore and Michigan Southern) takes advantage of the gradeless south shore of Lake Erie. With but one exception, the subsidiary lines were almost as gradeless as the main line. This one (Boston and Albany) and the entire impact of terrain on locomotives will be discussed after we give a brief history of the System.

Fine mood shot here. Lone Nash automobile witnesses train No. 13, New England Wolverine, passing Ashland, Mass., with K6a Pacific No. 594. The date is August 11, 1928.

MOHAWKS ALL The giant spirit of a Mohawk warrior looks down on a New York Central Mohawk locomotive racing along side the Mohawk River.
24x30" oil by Ron Johnston and Al Staufer,
Leo Cesareo collection

About a hundred years after Columbus discovered America, there was created from five Indian nations a model republic known as the Iroquois Confederacy. They (Mohawk, Oneidas, Onondagas, Cayugas and Senecas) lived in central New York State around the Mohawk Valley.

"Elder brothers" of these "Romans of the New World" were the mighty Mohawks. They were polite, shrewd, brave, and loyal, but still possessed the characteristic of being cruel beyond belief.

The New York Central System, as it existed at the time of the Hudson, was primarily the achievement of two men, "Commodore" Cornelius Vanderbilt and his son William Henry Vanderbilt. While the nine small railroads, stretching from Albany to Buffalo, were merging to form the original New York Central (1853), Commodore Vanderbilt was gaining control of the Hudson River Railroad. In 1867 Vanderbilt forced a merger of the two roads by simply refusing their freight (they made the fatal mistake of giving him cause for revenge) at Albany, and two years later (1869) the New York Central and Hudson River was officially organized. That same year (1869) the Commodore purchased controlling interest of the Lake Shore and Michigan Southern during the great stock market crash.

So in the lightning span of just two years, Cornelius Vanderbilt controlled the best rail route between New York and Chicago. The Big Four, Michigan Central, Boston & Albany, Pittsburgh & Lake Erie became "Vanderbilt Roads" in the following two decades by complex stock and personnel maneuvers. Thus was born the cohesive (mostly referred to as Princely) New York Central Lines.

IMPORTANCE OF TERRAIN

Now back to the importance of terrain or topography. On any railroad, **it dictates motive power policy**. There are two basic approaches: one is to build locomotives for specific areas and jobs; the other is to build average sized engines and use them in multiples as needed. Each has its advantages and disadvantages. The first requires multiple sizes and varieties while the latter method entails greater payroll and engine usage expense. Pennsylvania Railroad was the most noteworthy exponent of average sized engines used in numbers where needed.

But lucky New York Central with its gradeless routes, had all motive power options to choose from. Its policy was always large drivered speedsters on both freight and passenger.

First dramatic evidence of flat terrain's effect on design was the 1855 vintage high wheelers designed by Walter McQueen for the Hudson River road. Imagine; a 27 ton locomotive with 84″ drivers. Hudson River had them.

Things settled down for about the next 30 years with the bulk of the locomotives being 4-4-0's with drivers that seldom exceeded 70″ in diameter. Maybe the "old man" (Commodore Vanderbilt) had a hand in this. His "no nonsense" approach had already put a stop to multi-colored engines. "You can have any color you want just so it's black", and Commodore said it long before Henry Ford. Could just very well be that he pulled the plug on these fancy high steppers too.

Cornelius Vanderbilt.

William Henry Vanderbilt.

Keith Buchanan collection

Hudson River's Columbia.

17

American Locomotive Co.

897, built by Schenectady in November, 1891, had 19 x 24″ cylinders, 78″ drivers, 180# steam pressure and weighed in at a flat 60 tons. These were the pride of the road in the '90's.

BUCHANAN'S 4-4-0's

Now maybe it's just coincidence (we can't prove it) but soon after the Commodore's death in 1877 things speeded up again and this time for keeps. Dominating the scene from about 1880 to 1900 was NYC & HR's genius Superintendent of Motive Power, William Buchanan. His "I" class was to receive national fame and one, as we shall see, won immortality. Buchanan's I's were the first of what came to be known as the Central "look". With gray iron jackets (smokebox too), shiny black domes, natural wood cabs, and an almost religious "straight through look", they were aesthetically perfect. Perhaps a more accurate phrase would be "slavish devotion to horizontal lines."

Buchanan's 4-4-0's performed brilliantly, so he stuck (some say too long) with that wheel arrangement. Out on the Lake Shore (main line west of Buffalo) the 90's saw a transition to the 4-6-0 Ten Wheelers. Interesting; even though the Lake Shore was under Vanderbilt control since 1869, it was run quite independently. So "good kings" leave well enough alone and really, the name of the game is Run Trains.

999

It is true, certainly in part, that "times make the man". Can it be equally true the "times make the locomotive"? Probably so, for we have all the ingredients save one, for the building of the most famous locomotive in the world! The missing ingredient was simply the idea, or the man with it. We already have the railroad, the motive power potential and perhaps most important of all, a mid-Victorian worship of speed.

Our hero, former patent medicine salesman, was little George Henry Daniels, now General Passenger Agent for the NYC & HR. His idea was simply this: let's build a special engine that will take man over 100 miles per hour. Cornelius Vanderbilt II, grandson of the Commodore, and president Depew bought the idea and we won't even tell you what Buchanan's reaction was.

A few months later, the most famous locomotive in the world rolled out of Central's West Albany shops. There she stood, with gigantic 86″ drivers, 'Empire State Express' in silver script on her tender and No. 999 on her cab and sand dome.

She "did her thing" with a special 4 car train on May 10, 1893 just west of Batavia, New York, with Charlie Hogan on the throttle and Al Elliott on the shovel. She scorched the ballast at 112½ m.p.h. With a slight nudge from publicity genius Daniels, the famous New York Central became even more so.

New York Central · New York Central · New York Central

George H. Daniels. · William Buchanan. · Charles Hogan.

Here is the most famous locomotive in the world (999) raising some very real dust. The smoke was dubbed into the photograph later.

Great ten wheeler for the great Lake Shore. 80" drivered 602 was built by Brooks in 1899.

1900 NEED OF POWER

999 was the last hero. Fact is, the 4-4-0 had had it. At the turn of the century cars were getting heavier and schedules shorter. What was needed was power. You get power with weight and steam, and you get steam with fire. There just was no way to squeeze any more from the American with their tiny firebox between the drivers.

What emerged on the Central was this; Lines East (NYC & HR) developed the 4-4-2 type with a large firebox over the trailing truck and Lines West (LS & MS) favored the 4-6-0 Ten Wheeler with a long firebox between the rear drivers. The turn of the century saw an explosion in demands and subsequent locomotive development. Also, the golden days of individuality were drawing to a close. System-wide power procurement policies were here with all shots and game plans coming from New York City.

TWENTIETH CENTURY LIMITED

Before discussing this new breed of iron horse that culminated in the Hudson, let's turn to our little passenger agent and what just has to be his most brilliant creation. In the late 80's and early 90's both the Pennsy and Central did a bit of play with through limiteds (New York-Chicago) and special trains. None was of lasting duration, purpose usually being some grand fair or exhibit. Once again the time was ripe for something permanent so in 1897 Central inaugurated its first full-time through limited, called the "Lake Shore Limited".

Five years later, with sufficient motive power available to do the job, Daniels prevailed upon the "powers" for his new train. It was to be all Pullman, all plush and all fast, running on a schedule of 20 hours. And it was to be called (oh that little genius) "Twentieth Century Limited". Management was sold, so on June 15, 1902, two trains (one from Chicago—the other from New York) raced towards each other and thus was born **THE MOST FAMOUS TRAIN IN THE WORLD**. This as we shall see, played a vital role in the Hudson story.

TRAILING TRUCK

Steam locomotive development unfolded like a series of chapters in a book with the division points being some area in time or some startling mechanical discovery. 1855 is generally considered to be the line between the American Standard 4-4-0 and the 4-4-0's of archaic development. The "American" period reigned for almost 45 years, which was the longest in history. The turn of the century ushered in two decades of the "big engine". The invention (or development) of the trailing truck enabled it to happen. No longer was fire size limited to the cramped space between the frame. With the trailing truck supporting the firebox you could build just about all the locomotive you cared to out in front. The big firebox was "in" even on engines without trailing trucks. On Ten Wheelers and switchers they either hung the firebox back on the frame or suspended it above the rear drivers.

2-6-2 PRAIRIE

First Central engine with trailing truck was the 2-6-2 Prairie types, class J40a, No. 650 built in 1900 for the Lake Shore. Grate area was 48.6 ft. and drivers 81". These early Prairies looked as tipsy as they rode. There simply wasn't enough engine hanging out over either end of the drivers. They were disproportionately high and short, but still, a total of 81 were built. The last 35 (class J41) were 7' longer and had smaller 79" drivers, thus eliminating the bad riding qualities. All of the J41's were later built into conventional 4-6-2 Pacifics. One could rightly ask; why were they built in the first place? Probably because they were superior to the Lake Shore's Ten Wheelers so they simply stuck with them. We have observed other cases of Victorian loyalty in railroad policies.

4-4-2 ATLANTICS

In 1901 Schenectady built the first 4-4-2 for the New York Central. The Atlantics were good solid performers with almost 300 being built over the next seven years. No small amount even for the gigantic New York Central. They were pretty well scattered on all lines with the concentration on the NYC & HR (Lines East). With these later 2-6-2's and 4-4-2's we have the emergence of the standard driving wheel diameter of 79" for most passenger power till the end of steam on the NYC. The advantages of standardized driver size is obvious, with its interchangeability of tires, and in some cases wheels. The reason for the Atlantics relatively short lifespan on the New York Central (or anywhere in the USA) was the emergence and dominance of a new class steam locomotive, the 4-6-2 Pacific.

No. 3000, 4-cylinder compound with two inside high pressure cylinders powering front axle and low pressure outside driving the rear. Engine was built in 1904.

Lake Shore Prairie was later rebuilt into conventional 4-6-2 Pacific type.

Big Four Atlantic with their typical decorated flair stack.

EARLY PACIFICS

The six coupled (drivered) Pacific was perfect, at least for the next two decades. They were bigger than anything heretofore and firebox supported over the trailing truck generated all the steam needed to power the trains of the times. As trains grew, so did the Pacifics, until they reached their maximum practical power output in the mid 1920's.

First Pacifics on the New York Central were ten for hilly Boston and Albany (nos. 2700-2709, class K1) and five for the NYC & HR (2795-2799, class K) all built in 1903. By 1906, Michigan Central and the Big Four (Cleveland, Cincinnati, Chicago and St. Louis) had them. These early Pacifics had the same general specifications; 75" drivers, 50.2 sq. ft. grate area and engine weight about 215,000 lbs. All had Stephenson valve gear (inside the frames) piston valves and boilers as straight as a die. They looked lacey and light by later standards but were real brutes for their days, handling the passenger train quite well, but soon, not well enough.

K2 PACIFICS

It's the same story all through the development of the steam locomotive in America—"greater demands meant greater engines". In 1907 the first of almost 200 class K2 Pacifics were built, the first going to the Lake Shore. These, at least in appearance, were of the new breed with huge conical boilers, 79" drivers and outside Walschaert valve gear. They were designed by J. F. Deems (General Supt. of Motive Power - NYC & HR) and built by American (Schenectady). Their grate area was almost 57 sq. ft., which provided ample fire for the huge boiler. At 45 m.p.h. they developed 2000 cylinder horse power. The vital ingredient was there — steam and plenty of it.

THE SUPERHEATER

Around 1910, there appeared a new development so magnificent that it was literally getting something for nothing. If you installed one in an existing locomotive you would get a 20% increase in efficiency and with no increase in fuel consumption. This marvel was called a SUPERHEATER and its application and theory are ridiculously simple. You merely HEAT the steam which in turn gives you superior thermal efficiency (expansion qualities). Its discovery was supposedly by an old German who became apprehensive about power loss because of the distance between his boiler and steam engine in severely cold weather. To correct the situation he built fires under his exposed steam pipe. The old Dutchman was startled to see his engine run better than ever before. Thus was born one of the ablest servants of mankind (power plants and ships use them today). Its application on a steam loco was achieved by rerouting the steam back through the fire tubes before it went to the cylinders. Almost immediately after its discovery, all new locomotives had it and many older engines had it installed when pulled from service for class 1 repairs. Some non-road engines (switchers, transfer, etc.) used saturated (wet—not superheated) steam till the end.

K3 PACIFICS

Central's new passenger haulers, and first to be built with superheaters, were the class K3 Pacifics. They first appeared in 1911 and were built till 1925 with each subclass showing minor improvements and dimensional changes. In all 281 K3's were built ranging from classes K3a to K3r. The K2 and K3's were identical in all major dimensions but the K3's (with superheaters and other improvements) developed 16% more draw bar pull at 50 m.p.h.

Since runs of the time seldom exceeded two divisions, tenders of the K3's were quite small. Enough coal could be carried to make it from—say—Buffalo to Syracuse. Water capacity on New York Central tenders was relatively light since it was picked up "on the fly" from track pans. Exceptions would be the Big Four, the Boston and Albany. Tenders for those roads were built without water scoops. Incidently, track pans were evolved by Buchanan, first successful installation at Montrose, N.Y. on the Hudson Division.

BOOSTERS

A major improvement added to the later built K3's was the booster engine. The booster, invented by New York Central executive Howard L. Ingersoll, was a small two cylinder steam engine geared to the trailing truck axle. (It was first applied to 4-6-2 K11e, 3149) Its use was limited to lower speeds — starting trains and pulling grades. In both these circumstances, plenty of steam is available for the booster. The booster was a gadget, and like all gadgets had to be used correctly to achieve beneficial results. Old timers were skeptical, but then they were skeptical of the superheater too. In addition to adding about 10,000 lbs. tractive effort, it cut engine wear and helped fuel economy by allowing the locomotive to start at partial cut-off instead of full stroke (steam admission for only part of the power stroke). They were ideal for use on the New York Central's water level route. Just helped start 'em and the high drivers took over from there.

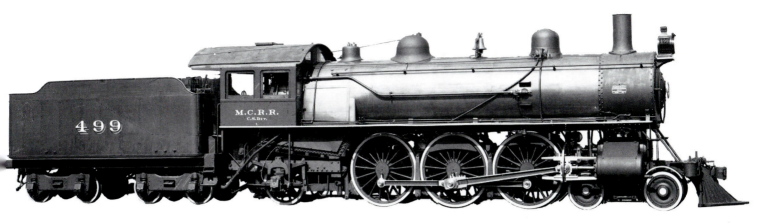

Schenectady 1904, 22 x 26 cylinders, 75" drivers, 200# pressure, 50.2 sq. ft. grate area, and engine weight of 221,000 lbs. Note typical straight boiler.

2703 was one of the first Pacifics built for the New York Central. Dimensions same as 499 - above, except cylinders 21 x 28".

4890, Schenectady 1910. Class K2L 22 x 28 cylinders, 79" drivers, 200# pressure and weight of 262,000#.

Schenectady 1923, 23½ x 26" cylinders, 79" drivers, 200# pressure, 56.5 sq. ft. grate area and weight of 295,500 lbs. Booster equipped. 3267 is representative of the last K3 Pacifics built in quantity.

Big Four Pacific, 6470-K3L, leaving Mattoon, Ill. with train #39, the "Missourian" on February 21, 1929.

J. H. Westbay

K2a 4843 runs through typical Lake Shore scenery probably somewhere in Ohio or Indiana.

THE FABULOUS RUN OF 3334

Central's management was well aware of the financial benefits, through locomotive utilization, of running engines over several divisions instead of just one or two. In Sept. 1924, K3q 3272 had just completed 211,637 miles without general repairs. Quite a record by any machine—any time.

In 1925 it was decided to pull a locomotive from stock and make a round trip run from Harmon to Chicago and back. That was quite an adventure for the time. On Sept. 10, 1925, Pacific K3n was readied at Harmon and coupled to No. 19, the Lake Shore Limited. 3334 was built in 1918 and had no stoker and no booster. Detailed records of the runs were kept, giving us a rare glimpse into the past.

We will detail them here:

1. Harmon to Albany, 378 scoops of coal, grates not shaken, rake not used.
2. Albany to Syracuse, 530 scoops of coal, grates not shaken, rake not used.
3. Syracuse to Buffalo, 384 scoops of coal, grates not shaken, rake not used. Coal taken at Waynport.
4. Buffalo to Cleveland, 603 scoops of coal, grates were shaken, rake not used.
5. Cleveland to Toledo, 341 scoops of coal, grates shaken twice, rake not used.
6. Toledo to Elkhart, 378 scoops of coal, grates shaken once, coal taken at Mina, ashpan dumped (first since Harmon).
7. Elkhart to Chicago, 256 scoops of coal, 60 scoops used to take train to Root St. engine house.

Normal lubrication was used on the run and the fire carried extremely light, so light that upon arrival at all division points there were spots in the firebox where ash was plainly visible. Motive power experts agree that this kind of "right" firing was responsible for the record run. Coal consumption for the 930 mile trip was 21¾ tons.

After a 12 hour lay-over, 3334 was coupled to the 11 car Lake Shore Limited (No. 22) for the run back to Harmon. The Eastbound trip took 27 tons of coal.

Only one trip was scheduled but after 3334 arrived back at Harmon in such excellent shape it was decided to repeat the entire round-trip. This they did and when the little K3n returned to Harmon on Sept. 16th they were proclaiming her "more famous than 999". Perhaps what she did was more solid, but little George H. Daniels wasn't around with his magic touch. Incidentally, all runs were on time.

K3d (Alco 8-1912) at Harmon, N.Y., October 22, 1932.

HARMON NIGHT

Harmon at Night. K3 waits with W/B Peekskill or Poughkeepsie local. Good solid time exposure here. No artificial flash bulbs. Note lantern path at far right.

Al Staufer collection

Edward L. May

Engine 4701 (ex. 3301) on train #148, Poughkeepsie Local, at Manitou, New York, July 2, 1939. K3p handles 5 car train with ease.

Al Staufer collection

K3g 4851 was built by Schenectady in 1913. We like these pre-refined K3 Pacifics; no boosters and fine archaic double cab windows.

Al Staufer collection

A new train to St. Louis just like the Century

NEW YORK CENTRAL LINES announce the inauguration on April 26 of a new de luxe New York — St. Louis service

The Southwestern Limited

"Just like the Century"
CLUB CAR
OBSERVATION CAR
COMPARTMENTS
STENOGRAPHER
LADIES' MAID
BARBER VALET
MARKET REPORTS

This all-Pullman, observation-car train, with equipment and service identical with the famous 20th CENTURY LIMITED, will leave New York every afternoon at 4:45 p. m. and arrive in St. Louis the next afternoon at 5 o'clock, in ample time to connect with trains to the Southwest.

The new eastbound SOUTHWESTERN, with the same complete equipment, will leave St. Louis at 9 o'clock in the morning and arrive in New York the next morning at 10:50 o'clock.

Southwestern Limited
WESTBOUND
Lv. New York 4:45 p. m.*
Lv. Boston 2:00 p. m.*
Ar. St. Louis 5:00 p. m.*
EASTBOUND
Lv. St. Louis 9:00 a. m.*
Ar. New York 10:50 a. m.*
Ar. Boston 1:00 p. m.*
Standard Time

NEW YORK CENTRAL

een flagged 3280 pulls out of Harmon with Section of the
th Century Limited while 3282 waits to back on to next sec-
n. Engineer of 3282 crosses over to watch the action. And
rn, if it doesn't look like Bob Butterfield himself.

The great wooden coal dock at Harmon, New York, November 11, 1930. The unjack-
eted parts of a locomotive's boiler were too hot for ordinary paint so they were usually covered with graphite. New York Central mainline power was normally black
graphite but 3280 obviously has a generous swash of the more normal silver gray
color to its smoke and firebox.

K5 & K6 PACIFICS

But all was not well in 1925. Passenger business had developed to a point where most mainline trains had to be operated in sections because 12 heavyweights was the absolute limit for a K3 Pacific.

The problem was bad, particularly in the New York City area. On an average morning, between 6:30 A.M. and 9:00 A.M., about 30 through trains were due to arrive in Grand Central Terminal. Add to this the crush of commuter and local traffic and we have a situation that has absolutely no margin for delay or error. Locomotive utilization was critical. The job was being done, but barely. Things were stretched to the breaking point and everyone knew it.

Motive power men had anticipated some growth, but nothing like this. In 1924 they took delivery on an experimental super Pacific, No. 5000 class K5. It was built to the absolute maximum axle loading permitted by rail and track damage limitations.

Comparisons Between K3 & K5

	K3	K5
Steam Pressure	200 lbs.	200 lbs.
Cylinders	23½ x 26"	25 x 28"
Main Valve	14" piston	14" piston
Grate Area	56.5 sq. ft.	67.8 sq. ft.
Total Heating Surface	3769 sq. ft.	3,952 sq. ft.
Total Superheater Surface	839 sq. ft.	1,150 sq. ft.
Tractive Force (inc. booster)	40,610 lbs.	47,350 lbs.
Drivers	79"	79"
Total Engine Weight	290,000 lbs.	308,000 lbs.
Stoker	None	Mechanical
Feedwater Heater	None	Elesco
Horsepower at 45 m.p.h.	2,100	3,200

As the dimensions reveal, there was a substantial increase in power and weight with the K5. The motive power department certainly thought it would be sufficient for the needs of the Water Level Route. No one could have predicted those boom years 1922 - 1929.

It should be mentioned here that an "instant" locomotive is impossible. There must be substantial lead-in time for planning, engineering, building and testing. In this book we are writing primarily about passenger engines, but when you consider all the freight developments, the 1920-1930 period was a busy one indeed. There was so much overlapping that it would be safe to conclude that there were locomotives in all stages of development at all times during that decade on the New York Central.

Anyway, getting back to K5's, as was the usual Central practice No. 5000 was tested over the entire system. She performed well and 35 engines were ordered over the next four years for the Michigan Central, Big Four and P & LE. But NONE for the New York Central. In addition, the K5 demonstrated one important factor. The reason for disproportionately greater horse power over the K3 was the larger grate area relative to size of the boiler heating surface. This, in essence, was the key to the Hudson design.

Ten modified engines (75" drivers — short tenders) were ordered for the Boston and Albany and classed K6. After the J2 Hudsons arrived in 1931 these ten were transferred to the P & LE.

OTHER PACIFICS

To complete the story we will mention the other Pacifics acquired by the Central even though they had no bearing on the development of the Hudson. They were:

Class K41 — 35 Pacifics rebuilt from original Lake Shore 2-6-2 Prairies;

Class K4 — 10 Pacifics built for the P & LE in 1917 and 1918;

Class K11 — a series of 200 Pacifics built simultaneously with the K3 but smaller, (69") drivers for freight and commuter work;

Class K14 — 28 Pacifics rebuilt from K11's with larger 72" drivers.

We have missed a few but that covers the Central's passenger power from the turn of the century to the advent of the Hudson.

The great train sheds were another casualty of our socialized transportation age. K6a 590 leaves Boston on the 2:00 P.M. B&A. April 10, 1926.

While the first 4-6-4 Hudson was under construction at Schenectady, K5b 9240 rolled off the erection floor. This is our all time favorite Pacific type locomotive.

New York Central

K4a Brooks 1917, 23½ x 26 cylinders, 72″ drivers, 200# pressure, 56.5 sq. ft. grate area, 290,000 lbs. 9229 is shown new at the builders.

New York Central

K4a in later years after extensive rebuilding. Most visible changes are trailing truck with booster and headlight location. The K4's were strictly a P & LE machine and received the usual "fussing over" and nice striping.

New York Central

K4b. Brooks 1918, shown in later years all rigged for some sort of front end test. These K4's were not in the evolutionary chain of events that resulted in the 4-6-4 Hudson.

New York Central

K5b, Schenectady 1927, shown as built with a bit of the old downtown Pittsburgh in the background. 9235 appears a bit short or "stumpy". Or maybe the other photos received an assist by tipping the copy board in the darkroom.

New York Central

K5b, Alco Nov. 1926, 6507 shown here at Springfield, Ohio, May 15, 1935. The following year her number was changed to 4907.

Al Staufer collection

K5a 4929 was originally a Michigan Central engine. We are not alone in our praise of these K5 Greyhounds.

4920, another Michigan Central alumnus, sits under CUT (Cleveland Union Terminal) wires at Linndale, Ohio. October 13, 1940.

Al Staufer collection

33

Norton D. Clark

B & A K6b, 595, with a good load westbound with Toronto, Cleveland cars for mainline 21 and 2nd 21 the Toronto Limited. Train is passing the Boylston St. passenger yard in Boston. Second car looks outdated, even for this 1929 scene.

High green for 595, from the Boylston St. bridge in Boston at the B & A's passenger yard. The date is June 30, 1928, just a few weeks before the arrival of the first Hudsons. We wonder how the K6 will handle these 9 heavyweights over the Charlton Summit? Probably quite well.

Norton D. Clark

The Men of the CENTURY

THE pride New York Central men take in the 20th CENTURY LIMITED is no greater than the pride the New York Central management takes in these picked men of the organization, charged with the responsibility of operating this famous overnight service between Chicago and New York.

The CENTURY is more than a train—more than a thing of steel and steam and electricity—more than an achievement of American engineering genius. Through twenty-two years of continuous service, the 20th CENTURY LIMITED has come to represent the spirit of American transportation.

To the men of the CENTURY this standard bearer of New York Central service is a very living thing—a thoroughbred of the rails.

NEW YORK CENTRAL

L2a 2700

We close our chapter on the pre Hudson era with two seemingly unrelated items, pictures of the first L2a Mohawk and the memorials to Alfred H. Smith.

L2a 2700 exemplifies typical New York Central locomotive procurement procedure, which is: build a sample engine, run its wheels off in road tests, then buy your fleet. 2700 was built by American in March, 1925 and tested on the Hudson division. Her performance on revenue freight between Albany and Syracuse was so impressive that an additional 99 L2a's were ordered.

Native Ohioan, Alfred H. Smith, enormously popular top executive, was killed in a riding accident in Central Park

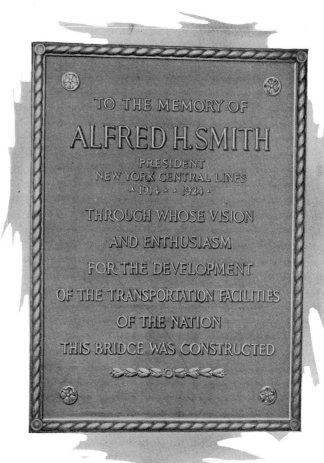

when he pulled up his mount to avoid hitting a lady rider directly in front of him. He was NYC Lines president for the critical decade prior to the development of the Hudson type. A. H. Smith continued the New York Central tradition of pouring back all necessary revenue into plant maintenance and improvements.

NEW YORK CENTRAL'S PRESIDENTS

NYC&HR	Cornelius Vanderbilt	Nov. 1, 1869
NYC&HR	William H. Vanderbilt	June 19, 1877
NYC&HR	James H. Rutter	May 4, 1883
NYC&HR	Chauncey M. Depew	June 17, 1885
NYC&HR	Samuel R. Callaway	April 27, 1898
NYC&HR	William H. Newman	June 3, 1901
NYC&HR	William C. Brown	Feb. 1, 1909
NYC Lines	Alfred H. Smith	Jan. 1, 1914
NYC Lines	William K. Vanderbilt	June 1, 1918 *
NYC Lines	Alfred H. Smith	June 1, 1919
NYC Lines	Patrick E. Crowley	1924
NYC Lines	Frederick E. Williamson	Jan. 1, 1932
NYC System	Gustav E. Metzman	Sept. 1, 1944
NYC System	William H. White	Aug. 1, 1952
NYC System	Alfred E. Perlman	June 14, 1954 **

* A. H. Smith Eastern Regional Director of U.S.R.A. 6-1-1918 to 6-1-1919.
** served till PC (Pennsylvania-New York Central) merger in 1968.

THE FIRST HU[D]

SON

New York Central

THE NAME

We all spend too much time punishing ourselves for missed opportunities, events and occasions that will never come again. Our salvation lies in the fact that once in a great while we have the presence of mind to seize the moment. Mine was in the summer of 1961 when I was introduced to Paul Kiefer, New York Central's superintendent of motive power, the man who was primarily responsible for the ultimate decision to build the experimental locomotive. We met at Grand Central Terminal, had dinner at the Biltmore, drank, ate and talked - talked - talked. In the context of my world, it was like an interview with God.

I shall endeavor here to quote to the best of my memory and notes, part of what Paul Kiefer said.

"The testing of 5200 was finally completed and the decision for fleet production made. I went up to the executive offices to see President (all lines) Pat Crowley but I had to get past Starbuck first. He wasn't going to let me by but I was persistent.

"Crowley, a gentle man, was very glad to see me. I don't think he ever knew how much Starbuck "protected" him. He (Starbuck) was really something.

The first Hudson locomotive with a string of 19 empty coaches, waiting for the day's test runs.

New York Central

The president of the New York Central Lines, Patrick E. Crowley, sits in the cab of the just completed experimental locomotive. A locomotive he was later to name. We hope he made the "Times" in this pose.

Darned if we don't really go for the way this machinery is put together. The cab-turret-heavy booster line - all of it.

New York Central

A memorable day, late in Feb. 1927 on New York City's west side. The new experimental locomotive is brought down for publicity photos and all round executive look over.

Second from left is Raymond D. Starbuck and far right is president of all lines, Pat Crowley.

5200

"Pat and I chatted a bit and we finally got around to the purpose of my visit. We talked about the new engine and her fantastic test records. I asked Pat if we should name the engine or if he cared about that at all. We were already calling the L class 4-8-2's Mohawks, after the Mohawk Valley and Indians. And then, I'll never forget that moment, he just looked at me; the sun was shining in from the West, it was late in the day. He swung around in his huge brown leather chair, away from me. He stared out the window for the longest time. He swung back and stared at me, his chin in his hand. Finally he spoke, "Let's call her the Hudson, after the Hudson River." I agreed immediately (not that it mattered) and that's how it was. The name stuck. It was a natural."

And that is how the most famous class of locomotive in the world got its name. We shall again refer to Paul Kiefer's quotes, but first, back to preceding events.

THE NEED

In the previous chapter we covered the growing motive power needs to 1926. Now we quote from a paper prepared by G. T. Wilson (General Equipment Inspector, NYC) in 1930.

"From operating statistics, it was found in 1924 that total train miles for the New York Central Railroad, which may be considered representative for the Lines, was 26% greater than that of 1919, with an increase of 33% in Pullman equipment car miles, whereas there was an increase of only 3½% in passenger car (day coach) miles.

"It soon became evident that the heavier Pacifics did not provide sufficient capacity in the operation of some of the heavier trains on the lines. Train loads were constantly increasing. In 1926 it was found that the passenger traffic was increasing in a greater ratio than provided for in locomotive design. With this increased tonnage of the Pullman equipment followed the use of observation and lounge cars, and service of two diners in certain trains, all of which greatly increased train loads. New fast limited trains were added. Schedules of trains were reduced.

"Prior to this progressive era, it was considered impractical to operate a locomotive over more than one division. With such practice the locomotive would be idle at a terminal one to three times longer than in actual service period. As a result of trials, the economy and increased efficiency obtained by operating engines over three to five divisions was soon realized. Such operation required the best possible inspection, maintenance and design to meet this severe service.

"Longer capacity tenders to eliminate coal and water stops for these long runs also represented an appreciable addition in engine loads.

"In 1926 the analysis of the train load and operating conditions, with the proper provisions for future demands, resulted in reaching definite conclusions that a passenger locomotive of entirely new design must be developed.

"The problem thus presented to the Equipment Engineering Department of the Lines was to create a design of locomotive with much greater starting effort, and a corresponding increase in boiler proportions to provide for increased cylinder horsepower capacity, with maximum output at higher speeds, but with weight distribution so limited as to keep the rail stresses and bridge loads lower than had been previously observed, the locomotive to be of such a design as to meet clearance limits for all parts of the Lines. Long contiuous runs required improvement in designs of wearing parts and a standardization for operation and maintenance over the entire system.

"The K5 Pacifics presented the maximum desired limit in weight for that type. Any increase in total weight required an entirely new design and wheel arrangement. After the preparation of several preliminary designs the conclusions were reached that the conditions could best be met by the 4-6-4 wheel arrangement and 79″ diameter drivers. Upon completion of general design, a complete diagram covering the major characteristics and specifications was prepared and an order for the construction of one sample locomotive was placed with the American Locomotive Company."

PAUL W. KIEFER

The difference between the intellectuals who built America and many of today's intellectuals (professional students) is that the former's theories and ideas were laced with the realities of hard work. That difference is enormous and is what gave this country its lasting, workable methods. They are literally the begetters of our Nation's greatness — these "brainwork" individuals.

Such a man was Paul W. Kiefer. Born in Delaware, Ohio in 1888, he began his career as a machinist apprentice on the Lake Shore & Michigan Southern; was successively advanced to Piecework, Construction Inspector, Erection Floor Machinist, Locomotive Designer, Dynamometer Engineer, Chief Draftsman, Assistant Engineer, Assistant Engineer of Rolling Stock, and then on January 1, 1926, replacing F. H. Hardin, became Chief Engineer of Motive Power and Rolling Stock for all the New York Central Lines.

When Kiefer took command, no firm decision had yet been reached to solve the passenger power crisis. There is always the "chain of command" and executive "courtesies and permissions" to be considered, but the ultimate decision to go ahead with the experimental locomotive was his, and his alone.

RAYMOND D. STARBUCK

To us, a mystery man, always present, and apparently all powerful. Why was he never selected president? Was he the REAL power during the Hudson years? We simply don't know. Wish we did.

Born July 26, 1878 Fort Ann, N.Y. — educated at Cornell — 1901 Cornell football coach — joined Michigan Central in 1903 in engineering post — division engineer year later — June 1912 special engineer to the VP and by 1915 special engineer to the president — May 1916 assistant to the VP and in 1917 assistant general manager New York Central Lines West (LS&MS). After WW I assistant VP NYC Lines — made VP operating dept. 1924 under Pat Crowley — 1932 Executive VP under Williamson — May 22, 1940 to Board of Directors when Walter P. Chrysler retired. Retired in Dec. 1947 after 44 years of service. Died at 87 in 1965.

To intimate he ran the railroad or otherwise wielded power beyond his immediate arena (as we have suggested) would be to disparage the men he served under, but the extent of his influence on policy decisions and day to day operations should not be minimized.

Robert A. Buck

Tanks full - blowers on - ready to go. A1 1416 and 4-6-2 #576 (K14g) about to depart West Brookfield, Mass.

LIMA'S A1 BERKSHIRE

The real technological breakthrough and actual predecessor of the Hudson was Lima's A1 2-8-4 Berkshire, the first locomotive in America with a practical 4-wheel trailing truck. Lima finished the A1 in 1924 and chose to test it on New York Central's Boston & Albany. Exactly why, we're not sure but since the mighty Central was a solid Alco customer, what better way to get one's foot in the door. The testing did result in some nice orders for Lima and the hills of western New England resulted in naming the 2-8-4 type, Berkshire.

To better illustrate the real significance of the 2-8-4 type, it would be well to compare their statistics with a previous (Lima built) NYC 2-8-2 Mikado.

	A1 2-8-2	2-8-2 H10a
Cylinders	28" x 30"	28" x 30"
Cut-off in Full Gear	60 per cent	Full Stroke
Boiler Pressure	240 lbs.	210 lbs.
Weight on Drivers	248,200 lbs.	248,000 lbs.
Front Truck	35,500 lbs.	29,000 lbs.
Trailing Truck	101,300 lbs.	58,000 lbs.
Total Engine	385,000 lbs.	335,000 lbs.
Drivers	63"	63"
Heating Surface Total	7,221 sq. ft.	6,358 sq. ft.
Grate Area	100 sq. ft.	66.4 sq. ft.
Tractive Force—Total	82,600 lbs.	77,700 lbs.

The first and rather obvious startling revelation is the "unimpressive" superiority of the 2-8-4. Is it really worth hauling around 25 more tons of expensive locomotive for a mere 5,000 lbs. increase in tractive force? On paper, NO. In actual operation, an emphatic YES. With abundant steam at higher pressure the A1 is able to equal the 2-8-2 power on only 60% stroke which helped result in a fuel saving

of about 20%. The real magic of the 2-8-4 lay in the fantastic ratio of firebox to boiler heating surface. With mechanical stoker distributing a thin fire over those huge 100 sq. ft. grates, the steam produced, was for all intents and purposes, inexhaustible!

Needless to say, Paul W. Kiefer was most impressed with Lima's new machine. If a 2-8-4 is that superior to a 2-8-2, wouldn't it follow that a 4-6-4 be far better than an otherwise equal 4-6-2.

Dick Jacobs

Double header at Syracuse, New York has A1a 1403 and helping Mike H6a leaving east bound out of Dewitt Yards.. B&A's A1a Berkshires were every bit as gutsy as they looked.

K3q Pacific, built at Brooks March 12, 1923, at a cost of $61,200.00. Received new tender in 1927, experimental trailing truck, 1926-1927, received train control in July 1926. HT stoker in 1943, renumbered to 4284 in 1936, booster removed in August, 1951.

Multiply this times 4,000 locomotives and we have all shops working at full capacity at all times.

New York Central

Here is Hudson No. 1, fresh out of the builders, waiting to visit Manhattan for press and official viewing. Tender is pretty much stock K5 type.

PACIFIC 3284

K3q Pacific No. 3284 was fitted with a 4 wheel trailing truck from November 1926 to October 1927. And that's about all we know about it. Some theorize that it was installed to gain operating experience and others say it was applied to lighten the load and relieve track stress. In either case, it was a brief experiment that probably had little or no bearing on the development of the Hudson.

BUT, obviously, we will reveal our feelings on the matter. We vote with the track-stress theory. First, No. 5200 Hudson was already under construction. Second, Central already owned several 2-8-4's so had ample opportunity to view 4 wheel trucks in action. Third, the K3q's were the heaviest of the K3's on the trailing truck. Fourth, these were days of complete obsessions with track damage — and probably rightly so.

We quote again from paper of G. T. Wilson written in 1930. "The single axle trailing truck presented a rather serious problem, as the weight of the Pacifics was increased. This isolated load may develop an unusually high rail stress, due to the fact that the rail, when considered as a continuous beam, tends to deflect in an upward direction at a point between the position of the back driver and the trailing wheel." He continues, speaking of the Hudson, "Account of the improved weight distribution of the locomotive, especially that of the drivers and trailing truck, a great improvement was found in the riding qualities."

PREVIOUS HUDSON PLANS

The reason we stress the "machine" over fact that it was the first 4-6-4, is that other roads were already planning Hudsons. The breakthrough of Lima's A1 assured that more 4 wheel trailing trucks would surely follow. It simply had to be! Fireboxes were getting bigger; way beyond the carrying capacity of the single axle trailer.

Design engineer C. H. Bilty and Chief Mechanical Officer L. K. Sillcox of the Milwaukee Road submitted preliminary 4-6-4 specifications to both Baldwin and American Locomotive Co. in 1925. A shortage of funds delayed their efforts till 1929 when Baldwin built their 4-6-4 class F6. So, by rights, Milwaukee Road should have been first with the 4-6-4. We suspect that all three builders were deep into the development stages of this wheel arrangement. Anyway, the fact that New York Central was "first" was merely a matter of circumstance, and not through years of toil, research and development.

HUDSON NO. 1

Paul Kiefer became Chief Engineer of Motive Power and Rolling Stock for all the New York Central Lines on January 1, 1926. Almost immediately thereafter the decision was made to proceed with the 4-6-4 experimental locomotive. Builder was to be "on line" American Locomotive Co., who built over 80% of all Central's engines.

The princely New York Central needed a new passenger engine and all-hands "turned-to", and we mean **all** hands. The entire year of 1926 was one of feverish activity involving not only Alco and NYC but ALL locomotive auxiliary suppliers. We are not exactly sure who did this, and who did that. Actually, most of American's (later name Alco) locomotives, even those built for Western Roads, looked like New York Central's anyway. The two are synonymous.

Construction was begun late in 1926 and the finished locomotive was officially christened on St. Valentine's Day, 1927. The only mechanical surprise in 5200 was the lack of combustion chamber. Otherwise she contained each and every mechanical improvement available at that time.

Somehow it seems right to us, that as 5200 burst through the red, white, and blue paper drapes into the light of day, her first glimpse of the outer world was a deep covering of snow. She best get used to it right off, cause the glorious Water Level Route runs through the heaviest "snow belt" in the entire United States. Many a time, the "Pennsylvania Limited" would be sweeping through a clean Juniata Valley, while the "New England States" would be slugging through over two feet of the white stuff at Syracuse.

So as 5200 pants to a stop, her eyes, still not accustomed to the light, see a lady (complete with 1927 circa costume — less ukelele) crawl up on her pilot and take a clean left handed swing with a champagne bottle and crack her across the coupler lift. Appropriate words for the occasion would seem to be "I Christen thee Hudson" except that the engine wasn't named yet. We remain confident however that the words spoken were most fitting.

Following the festivities at Schenectady, 5200 proceeded down the Hudson into the 72nd St. yards of Manhattan for further showing. She was not, however, awarded the supreme honor of display in Grand Central Terminal. Remember, this was just an experimental locomotive; great expectations, yes, but still an experimental locomotive.

New York Central

February 14, 1927, Schenectady, New York, the first Hudson tears through the bunting, gets a shot on the pilot, then gets an official look over. The rest is history.

5200 has just run light to Harmon. Marker lights on pilot are for backing up. She was a good looker from the start.

5200

Firearms side view showing Walschaert valve gear. All Hudsons through J1c were built with this gear but all replaced with Baker in the 40's.

New York Central

Here are the major mechanical features of locomotive 5200:

Cast steel frame with bolted cross sections;
Cast steel cylinders;
Solid bearings on all drivers and wheels, engine and tender;
Straight boiler;
Delta Commonwealth four wheel trailing truck;
Larger steam passages than K5 Pacific but same size cylinder;
Walchaert valve gear;
Precision power reverse operated by hand wheel in cab which aided fine "cut off" settings at speed;
Maximum cut off of 86% — steam can only be admitted 86% of the stroke or less. Full stroke not possible;
No combustion chamber; tubes started just ahead of firebox. The chamber just ahead of the firebox was eliminated because of stay-bolt difficulties;
Auxiliary steam turret just ahead of cab which eliminated considerable piping in cab;
Type E superheater;
D3 Duplex stoker;
Elesco feedwater heater sunken into smokebox;
Elesco feedwater heater pump on left side of pilot. Excellent location just below heater;
Cross compound air pumps on right side of pilot.
Location of compressor and air pumps on pilot was necessary to relieve weight on drivers. It also relieved the stress to boiler when this heavy equipment is suspended there; (second air pump added at Depew Shop July 1928)
Two air tanks under left running board. None on right side;
Alligator (two bar) crosshead which was typical Alco. NYC practice;
Two cylinder, double acting, C-2 type booster geared to 51" rear trailing truck wheel;
Pierce automatic bell ringer;
Air operated whistle;
Cast steel pilot with drop coupler.

Over all appearance was pretty much dictated by necessity of low clearance and Alco-NYC devotion to horizontal lines. All exterior plumbing possible was either placed beneath lagging or jacketed over.

Tender was similar to K5 or K6 Pacific type. No attempt was made at this time to design special tender for 5200. Remember, the name of the game was TIME. 5200 was rushed to completion for road tests. 6 wheel truck Hudson tender replaced original small one on October 15, 1927.

Engine cost of $80,000.00 seems unusually reasonable, considering she was theoretically a one of a kind. Everyone was quite confident that 5200 would be the prototype for the "fleet" but NO FIRM ORDERS WERE PLACED until she did her thing on the road. Further, the coming tests were extremely vital in that they would certainly reveal minor flaws and areas in need of improvement.

New York Central

Forgive our emotion but we really go that 4-wheel trailing truck. As far as the low cab and covered turret are concerned well - we are addicted to it.

The turret is simply a live steam collecting manifold that is placed where it is so all controls can be in the cab. From this one collecting point, steam can be distributed to feedwater heater, passenger car heat, air compressors, smoke consumers, generator, coal pusher, injector, etc., etc., etc.

This is what it's all about! Trailing truck for the first Hudson, made necessary to hold up the firebox of 81.5 sq. ft. It was 56.5 sq. ft. on the latest K3.

New York Central

No. 5200

All shiny and new at West Albany yards just prior to being rigged with test apparatus.
   Lower right photo shows Elesco feedwater heater and pump. All other Hudsons, and later 5200 itself, had two air pumps mounted on the pilot beam.

New York Central

New York Central

New York Central

STATISTICS FOR 5200

LOCOMOTIVE	5200	K5B	K3Q
Wheel Arrangement	4-6-4	4-6-2	4-6-2
Cylinders	25 x 28	25 x 28	23½ x 26
Drivers	79"	79"	79"
Boiler Pressure	225	200	200
WEIGHT IN WORKING ORDER (full of water, sand, etc.)			
Front Truck	63,500	58,500	44,000
Drivers	182,000	185,000	194,500
Trailing Truck	97,500	58,500	57,000
Total Engine	343,000	302,000	295,500
Wheel Base Engine & Tender	95'11"	90'11"	78'2¼"
TENDER (Tender specs. are for permanent 6 wheel truck type.)			
Coal Capacity - Tons	24	16	12
Water Cap. Gals.	12,500	15,000	8,000
Total Weight Loaded	280,800	274,500	168,000
HEATING SURFACE (specs. in sq. ft.)			
Firebox and Arch Tubes	281	257	231
Tubes and Flues	4,203	3,695	3,192
Total Evaporating	4,484	3,952	3,424
Superheater	1,951	1,150	832
Type of Superheater	E	A	A
GRATE AREA	81.5	67.8	56.5
RATED MAXIMUM TRACTIVE EFFORT			
Main Engine Only	42,360	38,540	30,900
With Booster	53,260	48,500	40,600
Factor of Adhesion	4.30	4.92	6.29

New York Central

THE TESTING OF 5200

So you have your new locomotive; how do you test her accurately and completely? There are three basic test methods: Stationary Test plant, Dynamometer Car or, just put the new locomotive in service and compete against existing engine performance.

Since New York Central had no stationary test plant, they used the Dynamometer Car method. Starting in about 1916, the N.Y.C. put every pilot model engine through exhaustive tests of this method. So thorough were these tests that railroads over the entire country sought and benefited from their results.

Before testing could begin on 5200 she had to be thoroughly "broken in". On later roller bearing engines, "break in" was brief but this procedure was extremely delicate with brass bearings. Break in was started on local freights where speeds seldom exceeded 35 m.p.h. Their continual stop-start, forward-reverse movements were ideal for this chore. The latter part of the three week period, 5200 was put on local passenger hauls; again most suited since there were no sustained high speed runs. J1a was now ready.

Test train stops somewhere on the Mohawk division for the company photographer.
It looks very much like Paul Kiefer standing on the pilot.

5200 and test train of 21 cars and dynamometer car in tow eastbound on Mohawk division near Karner, New York. Note two men in coal pile.

New York Central did so much testing that we accuse (acclaim) them of being unofficial tester for all roads in America — except Pennsy, of course.

Absolutely everything was tested, fuel consumption, back pressure, cylinder horsepower, drawbar pull, engineer's pulse — everything.

New York Central

We quote Paul Kiefer on 5200 tests. "An important aspect of testing was continuity. To achieve this we had the same engineer and fireman on all tests. It was their permanent assignment for over four months. They were engineer Owen McEvoy and fireman "Stretch" Keller. They liked 5200 immediately and before the tests were completed we had a real love affair going between man and machine. It was their baby. Oh how they loved that engine. As the tests were drawing to a close they tried to work out some arrangement whereby they could be assigned 5200 on some permanent basis. They knew that was impossible — it was a gesture on their part to show how much they hated to give her up.

"Well, we tested 5200 like no other engine was ever tested before. Oh how we did test her. We thought we'd wear her out. On all tests I rode in the Dynamometer Car; calling tests, calling for speeds or brake engine resistance — reading gauges, etc. I don't think I rode the cab hardly at all but I did spend time up front (pilot) on the cylinder tests and boiler gauges. She did absolutely everything we had hoped for, and more — much, much more. The whole secret is steam. With all the steam you need, particularly at speed, you can do just about anything you want to.

"After the tests I went up to see President Pat Crowley and - - - "

The Dynamometer car is half living quarters and half test apparatus. Primary function of the car is to check the actual "pull" of the locomotive. This is accomplished by a complex hydraulic compression unit of enormous capacity, which transmits results to continuous recording tape mechanisms. The "D" car is coupled between the engine being tested and the load. This load or resistance usually consisted of a "brake" engine and a generous cut of cars. The brake engine could help get the test loco up to speed and hold speed steady at desired point by use of engine brakes.

The locomotive being tested was further rigged with a maze of pipes, dials and wind breaks so that it was beyond recognition. With this mass of technical gear and humanity aboard you could run your engine through any test conditions you wished. It could be worked at various speeds, terrains, loads, valve cut offs, etc. Absolutely everything could be checked — from horsepower to evaporation rate.. Nothing was overlooked.

Now we quote again from the papers of G. T. Wilson.

"The official tests for the 5200 were started in March 1927, and were conducted with the New York

John V. V. Elsworth

5200 and test crew at Minoa.
   Squatting in front: Dutch Matthews - chef, Joe Belgarde, A. Meister, Clayt Hewitt.
   Standing: George Spink - road foreman of engines, Paul Kiefer, E. L. Johnson, J. J. Anderson - brakeman, W. C. Wardwell - conductor, W. Gordon, Don Covert, Alex Lawrence - Franklin RR Supply, W. F. Collins, Stapleton-Duplex Stoker, George Hurley, John V. V. Elsworth, H. Wolven, Charles Parsons - D.S.M.P., Phil Agans - trainmaster, George Usherwood - supervisor boilers.
   Hanging onto grab iron E. Buckley, in gangway is fireman H. B. (Stretch) Keller, sitting in the right hand seat of cab is engineer Owen McEvoy.

Central Lines Dynamometer Car under everyday operating conditions, for the purpose of obtaining the operating characteristics and efficiencies as may be expected in ordinary revenue service.

"Test runs were made over the Mohawk Division of New York Central, Line East, between Rensselear and Minoa, N.Y., a distance of 140 miles. This division is representative in profile and operating conditions for the New York Central.

"Several trips were made with the train of 26 steel main line passenger coaches, including Dynamometer Car totalling 1969 tons, a twenty car train of the same equipment representing 1443 tons, and one round trip with 15 sleepers, a train of 1083 tons.

"The results showed that the "Hudson" locomotive exceeded the expectation of design and performance of all other Lines locomotives ever tested for thermal efficiency, maximum horsepower, fuel and water consumption per horse power, and weight per horse power.

"The following tabulation presents the more important items of the test for the Hudson and K5 Pacific.

	J1a	K5 Pacific
Weight per pair drivers - lbs.	60,600	61,660
Maximum starting effort	46,500	40,000
Theoretical rated starting effort including booster	53,260	48,500
Maximum indicated horse power	4,075	3,890
at piston speed ft./min.	1310.76	1072.44
at M.P.H.	66	54
Engine weight per indicated H.P. (lbs.)	84.1	94
Drycoal per I.H.P. (lbs.)	1.91	2.19
Steam per I.H.P.	15.52	15.42
Average evaporation per lb. drycoal	8.15	7.24
Average combined efficiency of boiler, feedwater heater, and superheater - %	79.60	70.60
Average thermal efficiency at the Draw Bar - %	6.32	5.17

"The J1 produced 16% greater actual maximum starting tractive effort, without booster, over the K5, 27% greater cylinder horsepower at 22%

59

higher rate of speed. For overall thermal efficiency at the drawbar, the J1 showed an increase of 22% over that of the K5 and a decrease of 11% in weight of total engine per cylinder horse power."

The evidence was in. The fleet was on order.

Above: the steam engine indicator, the piping to the indicator and the indicator reducing motion mechanism.
Below: both sides of the actual card made on April 11, 1927.

5200

John V. V. Elsworth

John V. V. Elsworth

5200 at Rensselaer, June 2, 1927, after round trip from Rensselaer to DeWitt and return.
  Left to right: Mark Bromley - Alco, Alex Lawrence - Franklin RR Supply, Phil Agans - trainmaster, Owen McEvoy - engineer, Harry (Stretch) Keller - fireman.

5200 at old coal deck at St. Johnsville, N.Y., May, 1927, during capacity tests. Engine 3488 in the rear.

John V. V. Elsworth

New York Central

The testing of 5200 was one of the better recorded events in American locomotive history. Here she sits somewhere waiting for something.

61

HISTORY OF 5200

Temporary small tender was replaced with new type Hudson tender at West Albany on Oct. 15, 1927. New HT stoker was applied Feb. 27, 1935; cast steel engine bed, May 17, 1939; new firebox, June 12, 1939; booster removed July 1951, last major shopping was April 6, 1951, all at West Albany.

So after serving over 26 years on Lines east, ol' faithful No. 5200 was retired from service April 10, 1953. She had gone through such major rebuildings that little of the original steel remained that burst through that door at Schenectady on Feb. 14, 1927.

No. 5200

Star is only 8 years old and pretty much as built. Centrifugal pump, ahead of trailing truck, replaced the original pilot mounted feedwater heater pump. West Shore engine house, East Buffalo, New York, June, 1935.

R. Ganger

Edward L. May

Hudson No. 1 "swats-it" through Manitou, New York with train No. 40 the North Shore Limited, July 2, 1939.

Edward L. May

Only changes we can detect from original equipment are Pyle headlight in place of Sunbeams (we like Sunbeam better) and addition of Loco Valve Pilot.

Loco Valve Pilot indicates to engineer what the accurate valve setting should be (% of cut-off) at any given moment. Really handy, especially for the engineers who were not naturally born so.

Edward L. May

Now she looks like every other Hudson with Baker gear, air tanks on right side and marker lights gone.

5200 strays west to Cleveland, Ohio's Collinwood yards.

63

Central's 4-6-4's were water level flyers. Hill climbers they were not. Here 5200 gets a boost from an 0-8-0 switcher on West Albany Hill.

In my discussion with Paul Kiefer on Pennsy, he said "Our Hudson would have been a flop on their railroad and their K4's a flop on ours. They're just designed that way and cylinder size has a lot to do with it."

New York Central

THE J1 FLEET

Ed Nowak - New York Central

Somehow all the data and test results of the preceding chapter fail to fully explain or help us grasp the real superiority of this new engine. When comparing the Hudson and K5 Pacific, the ease at which the Hudson did the job is just as important as the increased power and efficiency.

Perhaps an analogy with the "known" would help. Assume we have two nearly identical new Ford trucks. One has a small 6 cylinder and the other a big V8 engine. Let's put a 20% heavier load on the V8 and run them at 70 mph up and down the super-highway 600 miles a day, every day. Now, which truck will do the job the easiest, cheapest and trouble free ? Everything else being equal, the V8 should win — hands down, more pay load, economy, and certainly on availability. This is how it was with the J1 Hudsons, running up and down the main line averaging about 18,000 miles a month.

Immediately after the 5200 tests were complete, orders for the new engines poured into Alco at a continuous rate. Hudson No. 1 proved to be a darned good prototype as subsequent classes of J1 had but minor improvements and most of these being developments of the time.

A meteorologist might help us explain that smoke lying back there, unmoved, staying right where it's put. Must be right temperature, humidity, atmosphere pressure and the content of the smoke (mostly exhaust steam) itself.
Engine is 5310 and mixture of cars indicates heavy War traffic.

Except for tiny lettering on tender these early J1b's were aesthetically flawless. Light graphite on smoke box was not general N.Y.C. practice. Two air reservoirs on left side looked great but one was eventually moved to the engineer's side.

Here are the main features of 5200:

J1a 5200 built in 1927
Walschaert Valve Gear
Elesco Feedwater Heater
Duplex Stoker
C-2 Booster
Automatic Train Control
Front End Throttle

Here is a review of the J1 fleet showing only those features — **not** contained on No. 5200. All these improvements are "as-built" only.

J1b 5201 to 5249 (1927)
Coffin Feedwater Heater 5201 to 5220 and 5240 to 5244

J1b 8200 to 8209 (1927-28) Renumbered 5345-5354 (8-1936)
8200 to 8204 Small 8 Wheel Tender

J1c 5250 to 5274 (1928-29)
Coffin Feedwater Heater
5274 BK Stoker
5265 to 5274 Thermic Syphon

J1c 8210 to 8214 (1929) Renumbered 5355 to 5359 (8-1936)
Cast Steel Frame with Integral Cylinders
Baker Valve Gear
Coffin Feedwater Heater

J1d 5275 to 5314 (1929-30)
Cast Steel Frame with Integral Cylinders
Baker Valve Gear
BK Stoker
Roller Bearing Engine Trucks (not drivers)

J1d 6600 to 6619 (1929) Renumbered 5375 to 5394 (8-1936)
Cast Steel Frame with Integral Cylinders
Baker Valve Gear
BK Stoker
No Scoop on Tender
Roller Bearings on Engine Trucks (not drivers)

J1d 8215 to 8229 (1929-30) Renumbered 5360 to 5374 (8-1936)
Cast Steel Frame with Integral Cylinders
Baker Valve Gear
BK Stoker
Roller Bearings on Engine Trucks (not drivers)

J1e 5315 to 5344 (1931)
Cast Steel Frame with Integral Cylinders
Baker Valve Gear
BK Stoker
Roller Bearings on Engine Trucks (not drivers)
Coffin Feedwater Heater
5343 SKF Roller Bearings on All Wheels, Engine and Tender except Engine Trailing Truck
5344 Timken Roller Bearings on Drivers and Tender, SKF on Pony Truck-Solid Bearings on Trailing Truck

J1e 6620 to 6629 (1931) Renumbered 5395 to 5404 (8-1936)
Cast Steel Frame with Integral Cylinders
Baker Valve Gear
BK Stoker
Roller Bearings on Engine Trucks
No Scoop on Tender
Worthington Feedwater Heater

Wilson Jones

A posed shot at Harmon, which was the basis for a very attractive color print marketed in the 30's. Looks just great.

October 1927. These "as built" J1b's were just as clean as a whistle. But as ALL steam locomotives got older they collected the gadgets of the times.

Schenectady, November, 1929. J1d had 25 x 28" cylinders, 79" drivers, 225 lbs. steam pressure, 81.5 sq. ft. grate area, engine weight 353,000 lbs., tender weight 306,400 lbs., and tractive force of 42,360 lbs., plus 10,900 more lbs. for booster engine.

Schenectady, June, 1931. 6620 (later 5395) was J1e built for the Big Four (Cleveland, Cincinnati, Chicago and St. Louis). Note, no water scoop.

Edward L. May

Every modern steam locomotive had two boiler feed systems, usually an injector on the engineer's side and a water pump on the fireman's side. Ideally speaking the water pump - feedwater heater system was used when working hard and the injector used on light demands like drifting down-grade or standing in a station. But things are not always ideal so crew would sometimes use the system that was functioning best, and on severe demands, both systems.

It's somewhat surprising that cost of the first J1b's ($87,000) was $7,000 higher than pilot model 5200. As the fleet was built costs rose to a peak of just over $90,000.00 per locomotive and tender. Two contributing factors were inflation and the increased equipment put into each unit. The impact of the depression directly affected pricing as the last J1's built (J1e), even though the most sophisticated, were the cheapest, costing around $81,000 each, but it was a darned-site easier for Central to come up with 90,000, 1929 dollars than 81,000, 1931 dollars. Allow us to dwell a bit and speculate on the unusually low cost of 5200. All we know is that $80,000.00 is what Central paid Alco. Since 5200 was such a team effort, it could well be that Central paid various equipment suppliers directly. Forgive our digression into the realm of finances as it has no direct relationship with running ability, but it is a part of the total story.

It comes as no surprise that as succeeding lots of J1's were built they became heavier, but to no great amount, totalling about 6,000 lbs . . (When comparing Hudson's statistics, we usually exclude No. 5200 and start with the first production model J1b.) The Hudson was purposely designed as light as possible to restrict track punishment and still do the job.

5200 had an Elesco feedwater heater pump on the left side of the pilot, and an air pump on the right. Since the next 20 engines built had Coffin heaters, this left room on the pilot for another air pump. The two air pumps were so well liked that they were applied to all remaining Hudsons including the J2 and J3 models. A centrifugal pump was used on all following Hudsons equipped with the Elesco heater. This pump was mounted low (below tender water level) on the left side, just ahead of the 4-wheel trailing truck.

All modern road locomotives had two boiler feed systems for obvious safety reasons. The Hudsons' other boiler feed was a lifting injector concealed under the right side turret covering. Since the injector used generous quantities of live steam, the feedwater heater "route" was most often used.

Starting with the J1c's, all Hudsons had one piece cast steel frames and cylinders. This created the greatest single weight increase (about 4,000 lbs.), but it was worth every ounce of it. Not only do you lessen the chance of breakage and stress fractures, but all things are in perfect unchangeable alignment. Roller bearings were applied to later J1's on the locomotive pilot and trailing trucks as these axles were particularly troublesome to lubricate.

J1d's and J1e's also saw the adoption of the Baker valve gear. New York Central had long favored Baker gear on their freight engines and the very precise, light Walschaert gear on their passenger locomotives. This introduction of the Baker gear on the Hudsons marked the beginning of complete system wide, total adoption of that gear on all power, both freight and passenger. Advantage of the Baker gear was excellent wearing characteristics and ease of maintenance.

Don't think that the engineers overlooked these various mechanical improvements when they designed the Hudson. Most of these features were simply

Edward L. May

J1e 5403 at St. Louis, Mo. November 13, 1937. 5403, former Big Four 6628, has Worthington feedwater heater and no water scoop. We like that monumental coal dock.

not available. In a sense, the J1 Hudson was a super modern machine that was five years ahead of the times.

Tender looks and capacity remained rather constant. Earlier J tender capacities were 12,500 gallons water and 24 tons coal. Later ones hauled 14,000 gals. and 28 tons. An exception was the first five built for Michigan Central. For some reason unknown to us, they were the 8 wheel K5 type. Maybe they had short turntables; maybe they didn't think they needed any more, and just maybe they were temporary due to production problems at Alco. In either case they didn't last too long.

The Big Four (Cleveland, Cincinnati, Chicago, St. Louis), with no track pans, had tender capacities of 15,000 gallons and 24 tons. Hudsons were assigned to various regions on the Lines. Engines would frequently get delayed but the policy was to work them "home" as soon as practical. Big Four Hudsons never strayed from home, and others seldom trespassed on their territory — no track pans you know. We are not above questioning management policies and certainly wondered why they just didn't build all J tenders alike. It's sort of like the cabless diesel fad of the 1950's. They were cheaper to build but there was just too much horsing around since none of them could be used on the point (lead).

External appearance of the 205 J1 fleet didn't vary a great deal, but there was some relocation and changing of equipment. The J1b's and J1c's had both air tanks on the left side. All following engines had one on either side. As is usually the case, the first built were the best looking. With air tanks on the left side, both running boards ran straight through; no steps as in later models. Cylindrical Sunbeam headlight, Walschaert Gear, internal booster exhaust all contributed to the J1b's cleaner horizontal lines.

Aesthetically, the J1 Hudsons were like something in between. They had the wheel arrangement and bulk of later, yet-to-come steam power, but their spoked drivers, serif Roman lettering and straight boilers added a "touch" that revealed their true lineage. It all hung together remarkably well; so well, that many (and certainly us) call them the most beautiful steam locomotives in the world. The later J3 Hudsons with their disc drivers and fat conical boilers seemed to suit the 4-6-4 type better, but the J1 remains the supreme classic.

Early in September, 1927, Hudsons began pouring forth from Schenectady in an endless stream. As soon as their break-ins were completed they were rushed into service, starting of course, with the top limiteds.

Again we quote G. T. Wilson, April 8, 1930. "In actual train service, the J1 handles, without difficulty, 16 to 18 car Pullman equipment trains on any of our schedules, including continuous runs, ranging from 403 to 925 miles.

"For eighteen trains westward on the New York Central and Michigan Central, several of which operate in two and three sections, these engines are required to perform under very exacting schedules. For the "Centuries", a through run for the engines is made from Harmon, N.Y. to Toledo, Ohio, a distance of 691 miles, making seven scheduled stops in 14 hours time between these terminals.

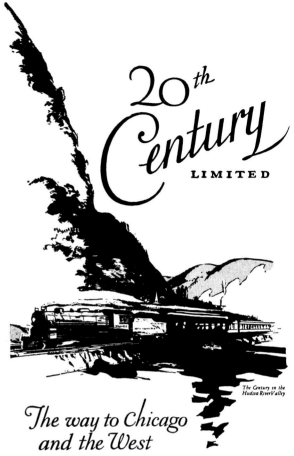

20th Century LIMITED

The Century in the Hudson River Valley

The way to Chicago and the West

Every afternoon at 2:45
from Grand Central Terminal
Twenty hours to Chicago

A new illustrated Hudson River booklet, with detailed maps, mailed free by any New York Central Lines Agent or by Advertising Department, 466 Lexington Avenue, New York.

New York Central
THE WATER LEVEL ROUTE··YOU CAN SLEEP

For reservations telephone VANderbilt 3200

View from Roosevelt Road viaduct on a scorching hot August 27, 1929 in Chicago, Illinois. Train is 2nd section of the 20th Century Limited and engine is J1b No. 5233.

Note LaSalle Street Station trainshed to right of signal and the absence of (not yet built) the familiar Board of Trade building.

A. W. Johnson

73

"Four trains westward are handled by J1 power from Harmon to Chicago, a distance of 925 miles in an average running time of 20 hours and 50 minutes, with an average total of 27 scheduled stops. The balance of the through runs are from Harmon, N.Y., to Cleveland, Windsor, Ontario, Canada, and Buffalo, N.Y., distances of 585, 655 and 403 miles respectively.

"In this service, a J1 handles 33 to 50% heavier trains and makes approximately 66% greater service miles per month than the K3 of ten years ago, as operated in division service.

"A year ago, a special section of the "Century", carrying a convention delegation from New York to Chicago, consisted of 18 Pullmans, weighing approximately 1450 tons. Although this train was allotted extra time, the results showed that the J1 made this run in 27 minutes less than the 18-hour schedule for the regular sections running time.*

* 18 hour schedule not inaugurated until April 24, 1932. We must assume he meant 20-hour schedule.

"These engines are meeting the current requirements of the Lines and all results indicate the reserve power available is sufficient to provide for future needs.

"Since September, 1927, 169 "Hudsons" have been built and placed in service on the New York Central, Michigan Central, Boston & Albany, C.C.C. & ST. L., and 5 additional are now under construction."

We emphasize the point again, "ease of doing the job" contributed to longer runs and availability. Two Hudsons could do more work than three Pacifics, and do it faster and better. This was the key to their success, not the slight increase in tractive effort or horsepower.

Each succeeding lot of J1 Hudsons was superior in some mechanical respect to previous engines of the same class. Obviously the newer locomotives were assigned the top trains whenever possible. The coming of the J1e's accentuated this policy. Not only were they (5315-5344) used on the "Century" when convenient, they were held and reserved for that service.

Man has yet to devise a more efficient way to move bulk materials than the steel wheel on the steel rail. Never was this more graphically portrayed than during World War II when the nation's Railroads hauled over 90% of all freight and about 95% of all inter-city passengers. This was the acid test for the Hudsons. It's one thing to haul 16 car limiteds under ideal conditions, schedules and maintenance. It's another to have all engines working beyond capacity all day every day. They did it, but barely. The Hudson was basically a "flyer." Well, for four

From any and every angle they were CLASS. One loss however was the removal of all front end marker lights on all Hudsons except those on the Big Four.

years, this "flyer" had the stop-start chore of trains that were too often, too long. Visualize a J1 with 20 cars, slowing or stopping for track repairs. It would be virtually impossible for "that" Hudson to make-up time. So it arrived at its destination a bit late; but it always did arrive. The Hudsons did it.

Because they were built just prior to a flood of innovations, the J1 Hudsons received more significant modifications and changes than any other major class of steam locomotive in America. This is conjecture on our part.

Edward L. May

On December 5, 1937, I was husking corn on our farm in Strongsville, Ohio. Ed May was out at Harmon taking train pictures. By all appearances, we'd guess they were using the washer this day.

In 1927, when the Baltimore & Ohio R.R. was 100 years old, they staged the Fair of the Iron Horse at Halethorpe, near Baltimore. Not only did they display all their fine locomotives and antiques, but they invited other railroads to show off their latest motive power. Here is New York Central's obvious contribution passing the reviewing stand.

Smithsonian Institution

75

In 1930, 5313 cost the New York Central $90,256.00. On Feb. 4, 1948, 5313 was sold to the TH&B (Toronto, Hamilton & Buffalo) for - - we wish we knew how much. Lettering, numbering and un-jacketed Elesco heater sure change the appearance.

Listed below are just the more prominent changes to the 205 J1 Hudsons. It is impossible to compile a complete "nut and bolt" record on every Hudson, so we can only mention those that we can verify. There were, certainly, more.

1) The first 75 Hudsons had original Walschaert gear replaced with Baker.
2) All, except Big Four engines, had marker lights removed.
3) Most, possibly all, had their booster engines removed. (Our records are incomplete.)
4) Many had original tenders replaced with the huge centipede type.
5) Many had roller bearings applied to engine pony and trailing trucks.
6) Many had roller bearings applied to tender trucks.
7) Most (could be all) received new stokers.
8) Most of the first 75 had original bolted frames and separate cylinders replaced with cast integral type.
9) About 35 (mostly J1b's) received new fireboxes.
10) Locomotive valve pilot added to all J1's.

The list could go on and on, but that covers the more obvious alterations. One change that was not made was feedwater heater. This is quite surprising when one considers that the entire fleet of 50 J3 Hudsons had their original Elescos replaced with Worthingtons.

The aforegoing list might give the impression that the J1's were not built "right" in the first place. Not so, for as we stated previously, they were built just prior to roller bearings, large steel castings, etc. And it was not uncommon for their monthly mileage to exceed 20,000. Since the J1's usually worked at 65% "cut off" with boiler pressure of only 225 lbs., metal stresses to rods and crank pins was due to enormous mileage rather than "thrust" or "kick".

The most complex aspect of running a steam locomotive, and that which sets it apart from any other of man's machines, is piston "cut-off". This one talent is what separated the good engineers from the bad. It had always been a "seat of the pants" or "feel" technique. Steam admission to power stroke was an endless variable, changing with each different speed and load condition. Its accuracy was imperative at the high speed range. Proper settings meant more economy, more speed and smoother running. Bad settings (usually too much steam to power stroke) were not only wasteful, but extremely damaging to the engine. If you "didn't have it" you could literally tear your engine to pieces.

To reduce the odds of human failures, the New York Central installed a device called a Locomotive Valve Pilot on all J1 Hudsons. Externally, it was a box-like apparatus, just below the reversing cylinder with arms or lines extending to the cab and reverse cam. It was a complex, magical device that could correlate the factors of speed and load and then correct valve setting. The engineer had just one gauge with two hands, a red for speed, and a black for valve setting. When the black was directly over the red, you were running at best possible cut-off.

All, or nearly all, booster engines were removed after World War II. The heavier limiteds could then be handled by the more powerful Niagaras, L4 Mohawks and diesels. The Hudsons missed them. Those "flyers" were in real trouble without that added assist in starting. We watched a "boosterless" J1

Edward L. May

The first 5 Hudsons delivered to the Michigan Central in 1927 had small 4-wheel truck tenders. We don't know why, perhaps it was turntable length. 8204 is shown in Detroit, Michigan in 1934.

J1d 5276 at Weehawken, N.J. August 20, 1949. Engine has Elesco, coil type, feedwater heater.

Edward L. May

Rare view of Big Four J1d with PT TANK. 5391 sure looks different than on the day she rolled from Schenectady as No. 6616 in 1930.
The more obvious changes are different tender, larger sand dome and stack, loco valve pilot, no booster engine and sort of a modified Baldwin rear driver.

Al Staufer collection

R. Ganger

If your time machine is all oiled up and working and if you like to be where it's happening then you'd be hard pressed to beat Wayneport, N.Y. most anytime in those glory years.

with centipede tender try to start a 15 car mail and express on a rainy night at Cleveland's lakefront. After taking up slack several times, they gave up and took a shove from one of the Alco diesel switchers.

The added weight of the centipede tender equaled that of an extra Pullman car, but it enabled them to make the 930 mile New York, Chicago run with only one coaling stop. Focal point of the action was Wayneport, N.Y., with its facilities built right over the main line. It was the railfans' Mecca, and no wonder. Imagine standing there on a 1945 evening when the Great Steel Fleet was due to pass. Not only was there constant action, but at times, Limiteds could be stacked up for several miles.

A Hudson would chew up about three tons of coal an hour, which was a respectable rate but thirst, like that of all steam locomotives was insatiable. All New York Central Lines had track pans except the Big Four and Boston & Albany. When passing over the pans the fireman lowered an air actuated scoop. The forward speed was sufficient to throw the water up into the tender. This force was so great that track pan speed limits were about 50 m.p.h. Anything in excess of that endangered exploding the tender sides. New scoops, developed in the early 40's, allowed higher pan speeds. When scooping water, a passing train literally "blew" the pans empty, but they had the ability to fill up in a couple of minutes as sections of trains usually ran five minutes apart.

The Hudsons were as human as any other steam locomotive, with their distinct personalities and idiosyncrasies. Most were excellent performers, but as expected, a few seemed prone to trouble and bad luck. They were complex. Engineers who ran them in pool service on the Toronto, Hamilton and Buffalo were always amazed at their extra gadgets, but more on this in other chapters of this book.

The J1's are gone. The America they ran in, is gone. How well I remember, the many times I heard them wailing through the night. Somewhere they are running still. I pray it is my lot to join them.

New York Central

It's enough that a steam locomotive is alive, has a voice that can chill you to the bone, but to top it all we have extras like this. Could our physical beings take the emotional stress to witness this again.
Taking water at Clinton Point, February, 1935.

Edward L. May

The Hudson tender was just as proportionately right as the engine it was joined with. The sheet metal plate (by coupler) was to deflect water.

Aesthetically abominable, on a Hudson at least, but functionally fantastic. Excellent weight distribution, tracked beautifully and only one coal stop was needed on the 960 mile run.

New York Central

79

Boiler front removed showing screening to catch the hot ash that comes swooping through the tubes after each enormous draft caused by the exhaust steam blasting up the stack.

New York Central

View of water scoop in lowered position at pit at East Syracuse. Inspector is holding oil flame to help detect air leaks.

New York Central

View from the engineer's front window. There was a feeling of security and safety with that long barrel out in front to protect you in case some car or truck decided to make a race of it.

Looking through the engineer's side window showing Duplex stoker. The deck and roof were wood.

New York Central

Inside that door is a firebox about the size of a small bedroom — 8′ x 10′.

Note heat shield on right side to protect engineer from brilliant flashes when the fireman was putting in a shot by hand.

New York Central

81

Two nice views of Big Four Hudsons taken at Linndale, Ohio, 5382 in November, 1937 and 5385, September, 1936. On 5385's tender we can barely detect where the big word SYSTEM and small C.C.C.&St. L. were just painted off.

5300 at Cincinnati, Ohio in 1951. Note how the poor girl is sagging by the cab. First and main drivers are Union Steel Casting's web-spoke style.

New York Central

General Railway Signals' Automatic Train Control. "An electrically operated device, attached to the locomotive and acting in conjunction with magnets, ramps or trips attached to the track; permits the control of, or the automatic stopping of trains in case of dangerous speeds or other unsafe operating conditions."

In the vernacular of the trade, "run a red block Charlie and you're shut down right now."

Excellent views of turret manifold showing control line going back to cab and steam heading out front end.

New York Central

Al Staufer collection

Standing Proud.

Train #41 leaving Harmon, New York. Photo was probably taken in the 20's. We consider these J1b's (as built) the prettiest of all the Hudsons.

Smithsonian Institution

Harold Stirton collection

5233 and 5265 with 17 car #14, eastbound mail. Invariably when we see Hudsons double heading, purpose was to balance power. Lead engine would have to raise scoop half way through pan or rear engine wouldn't get any water at all.

Second section #10 "Water Level Limited" leaving Englewood, Ill.; to left is second section of Pennsy's "Broadway Limited." October 3, 1937.

Harold Stirton collection

New York Central

New York Central

New York Central

These two pages and the two following are a series of photos taken of Hudson J1b 5216 at Harmon, New York. Just why it was this particular engine, we don't know. It has more striping than we've seen on any stock J1, so maybe it was selected for some special assignment.

5216 is clean but not new. It appears to be about a year old and is 'as built' except for addition of loco valve pilot.

J1

87

Staufer collection

Left, cyclops in the night, probably Harmon.
Above, probably Peekskill when they used MU's drawn by 4-6-4's beyond Harmon, the end of electrfication.
These negatives from my personal collection were taken by a New York Central Conductor who was more than a lens artist. He was a purist. No saccharine bulbs flashing here. Just set up your tripod and "let 'er soak in".

NIGHT

HARMON

West on Track 3. Harmon in twilight.

Al Staufer collection

IN THE HOUSE

— at Harmon, November 9, 1928. Sections were so usual they never removed flags from engines. And you can bet that 3281 at right was still doing some hot-shotting, too!

Al Staufer

Berea, Ohio is a hot spot on the New York Central. It's where the old Lake Shore and Big Four merged about 9 miles west of Cleveland.

5371 passes the tower eastbound down the old Lake Shore towards Cleveland's lakefront. Terminal bound trains branch to the right on the old Big Four before reaching this point.

New York Central

Famous Pair here. Ford Trimotor and J1b Hudson. Ford has little trouble throttling back to 85 m.p.h. for this planned run-by. Railroad's love affair with airplanes ended abruptly when it was fully realized the impact Uncle Sam's love affair with same would have.

Manhattan bound #132 "Henry Hudson", with J1e 5320 on point, rips through roc cut at Peekskill. In consist are Toledo, N.Y. coach, Syracuse, N.Y. diner lounge an parlor, and Detroit, N.Y. 12 section 1 drawing room-sleeper.

Edward L.

Al Staufer collection

Bellefontaine, Ohio, July 2, 1939. 5404 (ex. Big Four 6629) was not the last J1 Hudson built. 5344 was. Engine is equipped with the very efficient open type Worthington feedwater heater where the boiler feed water comes in direct contact with the heater's live steam.

Very rare shot here. As built J1b, except has Scullin disc main driver. Probably a test prior to using disc wheels on the J3's or - could also be an attempt to solve chronic main crank pin fractures.

J1c at Albany station, June 28, 1936. Another foreign main driver.

Edward L. May

THOROUGHBREDS

Edward L. May

Thoroughbreds on the ready track at Harmon engine terminal. That's not Bob Butterfield but it very easily could have been.
We'll take Ed's word for it as he was there — but Bob was noted for his very serious "oiling around".

A. W. Johnson

1930

POWER

A. W. Johnson

Any photograph of the late 20's and early 30's had a lot going for it, but Al Johnson was able to impart something else. It was mood, feel, genius — difficult to describe. What he shot was partly different because he wasn't afraid of, or partly favored, gray days, the way it really was. Too many amateur photographers are mechanical slaves to perfection. You can't learn soul. You're born with it — or not!

Both photos here show the second section of the "Century" leaving Chicago on different January, 1930 days.

CHICAGO SNOW

Three Al Johnson creations, all showing the Century leaving Chicago on January, 1930 days that just reek cold.
    A side thought on cold — we wonder about the variables of fuel consumption and performance between temperature extremes. We suspect it would be at least noticeable.

A. W. Johnson

A. W. Johnson

Washington St., Syracuse, N.Y., Sunday, September 13, 1936. Train is westbound #51 with engine 5282. Cripes lady, will ya' look up! That's the world famous "Empire State Express" about to pass you.

SYRACUSE

We like winter and we like trains so it's quite obvious how we rate this picture — Just Fantastic. Washington St., Syracuse, in 1932.

Central New York Chapter NRI

"Empire State Express" again. Line up of vintage cars is quite real as year is 1935-1936. And speaking of cars we'd take a nickel for every one scraped by a passenger car or locomotive.

New York Central

SYRACUSE

New York Central

The ladies are far more interested in the man sitting on the light pole with a camera than they are in these everyday surroundings.

The scene just reeks with nostalgia and glimpses into what it was like back in the mid 1930's. These were the days before suburban sprawl and resulting shopping centers and malls. Days when everyone came downtown. America was always a land of signs, but prior to the neon lights they were usually painted or lightbulbs.

This is the America of my youth and quite frankly, I like it a little bit better.

What the hell are they celebrating? Hard as it may be for a rail fan to grasp, they are whooping it up for the last train down the main drag, Washington Street. The Auburn and Syracuse ran the first train down Washington St. on June 4, 1839. So here it is 97 years later on a rainy day, September 24, 1936. It's all over and we must admit we don't see how they survived having all New York Central's passenger fleet run down their main drag.

Tracks were built right into the pavement like street car tracks and speed limit was a very strict 15 m.p.h. There were 68 regularly scheduled trains each day, increasing to as many as 125 train movements near holidays. The way we calculate it, that had a train on the street just about all the time.

Getting back to our time machine, I'd sure like to spend a day on Washington St., Syracuse, N.Y. — say about 1929 and watch the great steel fleet moving slowly by.

New York Central

New York Central

Clean car, clean locomotive, nice girls, but see the work-a-day overalls on the engineer or whoever the fellow is demonstrating the coupler lift. Car may be a Dodge.

The "in" ads today use jet airplanes for backdrops. In the late 20's they used the most famous class of steam locomotive in the world.
Lee overall ad. 5221 just might be brand new.

New York Central

J1

Another ad using a car, which we won't even attempt to identify. This does give us a nice view of Harmon, N.Y. coal dock.

New York Central

111

ALBANY

New York Central

5209 J1b standing on track #8, eastbound Albany Union Station. Edifice opened December 17, 1900 and considered a railroad classic. Crew is being photographed.

Spanking brand new J1b 5244 coming off turntable of newly built Harmon roundhouse. The blurred and whispy steam and smoke tells us this is a time exposure. Stop your camera and let 'er burn in.

Edward L. May

J1

Nowak - New York Central

taking water at Scotia, N.Y., just west Schenectady. Train is westbound.

When a locomotive comes in off a run it is put through a standard routine. It varies on some railroads but it goes something like this: inspection pit, ash pit where fires are usually dumped, coaling dock, sand, water and washing platform. Spraying equipment uses hot water or steam (or both) mixed with cleaning compounds.

New York Central

W. H. N. Rossiter

5253 on mail train near Athol Springs, N.Y.

"Knickerbocker" #41 wheels along near Peekskill behind J1d 5296. July 20, 1941.

Edward L. May

W. H. N. Rossiter

T.H.&B. 501 (ex. NYC 5311) on Canadian Pacific train #772 at Lorne Park, Ontario, Elesco coil heater gives J1 a very chunky brow.

Canadian Pacific's #772 (Buffalo-Toronto) behind T.H.&B. 502 (ex. NYC 5313 J1d).

W. H. N. Rossiter

Jim Seacrest collection

Elkhart, Ind. 1944. This is the way it was during the big war. American railroads hauled about 95% of everything, a truly herculean effort. So how does Big Brother and the cities of the Nation show their appreciation — by building a network of superhighways (now almost totally dominated by big rigs), by building jet ports and radar networks — totally publicly financed and by keeping a tight lid of controls on the railroads — THAT'S HOW!

Blasting along eastbound near Oak Harbor, Ohio. It was snappy cold out there.

Bob Lorenz

Local leaving Harmon for Poughkeepsie, N.Y.

Tom Mulaniff

118

New York Central

Harmon, N.Y. Yards, July 1928. Mostly Pacifics here. Hudsons were just starting to arrive. New roundhouse in background. Original house is out of picture to right.

Al Staufer collection

Inbound power awaiting the ash pit. Harmon, N.Y. about 1930.

Very-very typical NYC train somewhere on the mainline, about 1935. 5294 is hauling 7 mail cars, 1 combine coach and 5 coaches.

THE WATER LEVEL ROUTE

New York Central

123

Wayne, Michigan.

Ron Morse

Bob Malinoski

SNOW

St. Valentine's Day, 1951 has mail train No. 4 with 5320 and 5261 handling 13 cars and rider coach 185, Englewood, Ill. When power must be moved (balanced) to compensate for different east-west flow of traffic it is done as extra power on trains.

Blasting eastbound out of Peekskill, N.Y. station.

Ed Nowak - New York Central

SOUTHWESTERN LIMITED

Train #12, the Southwestern Limited, moving at about 70 m.p.h. near Pendleton, Ind. September 20, 1931 pulled by Big Four Engine 6618.
   Cornfield in background is nearly ready to be cut by hand and put into shocks.

Shades of Syracuse! 5335 with 2nd #33 moving through the streets of Springfield, Ohio.

Si Herring

J. H. Westbay

Ed Nowak - New York Central

5308 at Indianapolis, Ind. Engine at left rear is Big Four K5 Pacific.

Al Staufer collection

J1 leaving station, we're not sure exactly where. Appears to be New York area.

Ed Nowak - New York Central

Eastbound (south) limited about to pass through one of the rock cuts between Bear Mountain and Peekskill along the Hudson River

J1

J2's FOR THE

B&A

Norton D. Clark

New York Central Hudsons were built in three major lots:

1) 205 J1's 1927-1931
2) 20 J2's 1928-30-31
3) 50 J3's 1937-38

The J2's were a B & A machine, designed for that hilly road and the least "Hudson" looking of them all. Even so, they were virtual duplicates of the J1 Hudsons with two major differences. Drivers were 75" instead of 79", but frame spacing was the same so that the larger could be installed if ever needed. Tender was stock, small K5, 8 wheel type that held 16 tons and 10,000 gallons. The last 15 built had coal capacity increased to 17 tons.

Major Specifications of J2a-c (600-619)

Cylinders	25 x 28"
Drivers	75" (later 76")
Boiler Pressure	240 lbs.
Engine Weight	353,000 lbs.
Grate Area	81.5 sq. ft.
Tractive Force (with booster)	55,400 lbs.

J2c 616 heading the 2nd section of train #8 from Albany to Boston, at North Grafton, May 30, 1932.

Fireman's side view of J2c 610, new at Lima, Ohio. Large square sandbox applied August 5, 1936 at W. Springfield shops. Renumbered April, 1951 to NYC 5465.

Features of B & A Hudsons
J2a 600 to 604 built by Schenectady in 1928

Baker Valve Gear
Coffin Feedwater Heaters
Cost — $89,600.00
C-2 Booster
Automatic Train Control
Front End Throttle
BK Stoker

Features that differed from those above:
J2b 605-609 built by Schenectady in Aug. of 1930 — Cost $91,880.00
J2c 610-619 built by Lima in April of 1931 — Cost $80,350.00

We have no records to prove it, but we can safely assume that 600-604 had a cast frame, bolted construction, and separate cast cylinders. 605 to 619 probably had cast steel frame with integral cylinders. No tenders had scoops.

Their ratio of major rebuildings and changes was less than the fleet of J1's for two — possibly three reasons. First, they were built slightly later, thus had more improvements "built in." Second, they worked harder than the J1's, but it was virtually impossible on the short (about 200 miles) B&A to accumulate much mileage. Third, probably nowhere else on the New York Central Lines were engines so pampered and well cared for.

Changes after building:
10 received new HT stokers, 600-604, and five among the other 15;
All 20 received roller bearings on engine and tender trucks;
All 20 received Locomotive Valve Pilots;
14 received new fireboxes. This ratio is much higher than the J1's and probably reflects the punishment of pulling hills as opposed to running level.

Most obvious change of all, and the one that destroyed their looks was the application of huge square sand domes in 1936 and '37. No question, more sand capacity was needed for the hills, but that huge box absolutely did not conform with the lines of the engine, but like so many "uglies" in this world — you eventually get used to it.

Between 1947 and 1950 they were assigned to the New York Central and numbers and lettering changed from "600-619 BOSTON AND ALBANY" to "5455-5474 NEW YORK CENTRAL." In 1951 all B&A power was renumbered to N.Y.C.

J2c at West Springfield, Mass., November 2, 1932. Engine is about year old and unchanged.

Donald T. Hayward

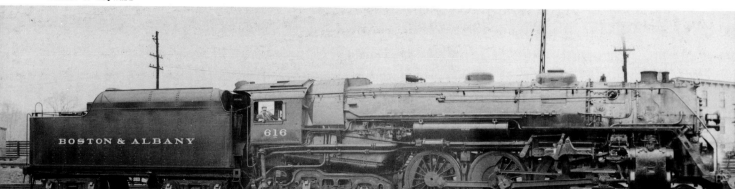

Schenectady, August, 1930, J2b 605. 25 x 28" cylinders, 75" drivers, 240 lbs. steam pressure, engine weight 356,500 lbs., tender weight 205,800 lbs., tractive power at 65% cut-off 44,800 lbs. (add 10,600 lbs. for booster.) Grate area 81.5 sq. ft.

As the N.Y.C. main line Hudsons were getting centipede tenders, the 12 wheelers they replaced were put on the B&A Hudsons. There was no precise sequence to this and often the larger tenders got to the engines before they were assigned to the Central.

One thing these "hill climbers" didn't need on the parent road was a booster engine, so some were removed.

Lima built the last ten (610-619) and were the only Central Hudsons not built by Schenectady. Why? We don't know. Locomotive orders were virtually nonexistent in 1931, and just maybe they did it to help them out. Big companies will do things like that.

On "looks", the J2's were fascinating partly because they didn't quite hang together. When we look at any individual face, we grasp the "whole". In other words we are immediately and subconsciously aware of the basic proportions, the abstracts of the face shape and various relationship of features like eye width, space between mouth and nose, mouth and chin, etc. This is what makes us look as we do. (Ask any portrait painter.) So it is with locomotives. We grasp the "whole." The unique factor of viewing the J2's is that we can't help but compare them with the more familiar J1's. With smaller drivers, short tender, and huge sand dome — well, they were just different.

The major appearance flaw (excluding sand dome) on the J2's was the relationship between cab and tender. On good locomotive designs there is a conformation so that when you look at an engine from the front or rear quarter, there is an undisturbed flow between them. Not on the J2's. The tender collar was higher and shaped differently than the cab roof. Might be that they used stock K5-K6 tenders and didn't bother to redesign the upper contours. Actually, the J2's looks were improved with the later applied J1, 12 wheel tenders that were specifically dsigned for Hudson use.

Another disappointing feature of the B&A Hudsons is that most had "drooping" cabs, particularly Limas' 610-619. Because of expansions and contractions, the only fixed connection between locomotive boiler and frame, is at the cylinder saddle. There is also a sheet metal support between the rear of the frame and the rear of the cab and herein may lie the trouble. Could it be that boiler expansion was so great on the J2's that it literally jammed the cab to the rear to be pulled down by the support plate.

Since we are not mechanical engineers it is our privilege to raise the question, propose a theory, but

609 taking water at Springfield, Mass. on October 12, 1933. Engine is as built including sand dome.

Norton D. Clark

not necessarily prove it. Anyway, the saggy cabs looked like heck.

All our ravings here about minor dislikes were certainly unnoticed by those who viewed them in the flesh. Reason, as we stated before, was — they were the most fussed over, prettied-up engines on all Lines, and just maybe the whole USA. They were always clean and wiped down (we're talking primarily of the years 1928-42). Graphite was periodically applied to the smoke boxes and boiler fronts were painted white. All trim and lettering was silver and if that wasn't enough, they were actually painted green. Yes green! We've heard about 28 different color combinations so who knows for sure which is right. Maybe all 28 are. The one we hear most (and it does sound quite logical) is, Pullman Green tender and cab sides, Brewster Green boiler and cylinder jackets, graphite smoke box, white face, all striping and lettering silver, and black running gear, cab roof and tender top. This may be only partially right as it stands to reason when you start painting engines two shades of green, differences are bound to occur. Paint on hand could cause variables as could man's innate desire to decorate and be creative. He's been doing it for 50,000 years to our knowledge, and who among us can say that roundhouse workers are immune.

Another point worth throwing out for conjecture is; why were the B&A J2's built in the first place? End to end run on the road was only 200 miles. Many runs were of partial trains that connected with main-line trains at Albany, seldom over 10 to 12 cars, and usually much less. B&A passenger traffic seemed to fall easily within the range of the K6 Pacifics they already had. Certainly the Hudsons could do it better, but were they really necessary? Must be, because the B&A got them. They, in turn, graciously exiled their K6's to the Pittsburgh area (P&LE). In the complex corporate structure of all N.Y.C. Lines, no road was quite as powerful and independent as the little B&A. We know of no instance where they ever got the short end of the stick. Quite the contrary — there always was a lot of money up there in Boston.

The J2 Hudsons easily did their work up and down their two big hills for their entire 20 year stint.

Edward L. May

5460 (ex. 605) at Weehawken, N.J., June 18, 1951. Loco valve pilot has been removed and tender coal looks like slack (dust).

5460 taking coal via conveyor at Weehawken, N.J., June, 1951. No cab sag on this locomotive. That wooden sand tower is a real big hunk of tomorrow's folk art.

R. Ganger

Edward L. May   612 at North White Plains, N.Y., September 1949. Small tank for Harlem Division.

607 in B&A service with J1 Hudson tender. Beacon Park engine terminal (Boston) September, 1947.   Edward L. May

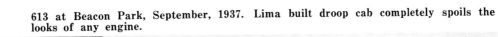

Edward L. May   613 at Beacon Park, September, 1937. Lima built droop cab completely spoils the looks of any engine.

612 storming up through the Berkshires crossing the Westfield River near Huntington Mass., with #25, the "Century", July 26, 1932. Club car, dining car, obs. parlor, Boston to Albany. The other pullman room cars will be dispersed to other trains at Albany for destination to Chicago, Cincinnati, and Pittsburgh.

Norton D. Clark

Al Staufer collection

There is only one major fixed point between the boiler and the frame (cylinder saddle) to allow for expansion. One other connection is the sheet supporting the cab at the rear and it's our contention that this plate pulled the cabs down on the B&A J2's. Theoretically then, contraction of the boiler should pull the cab back up again. Maybe this is what actually happened, or partly so.

Lee A. Hastman collection

Weehawken engine terminal again and that neat wooden sand tower. Big square sand dome is gone, replaced by a J3 sized one. Booster still remains and maybe the J2's kept them till the end.

Edward L. May

Crystal sharp photo of J2c at Chatham, N.Y. on #22 the Lake Shore Limited. About the only nice thing one can say about that huge square sand dome is it's sort of a B&A trademark.

J2

Steam drifting forward on port side helps outline loco from background, giving an already great photo an assist.
We wonder why they went through the expense of changing sand domes again. Time was running out and everyone knew it.

Edward L. May

Ed Nowak - New York Central

B&A J2a 600 coming off the Hudson River bridge entering Albany Union Station with a real dog local. Baggage car is wood and truss rods. Bridge can be found in drawing on opposite page.

NEW ENGLAND STATE

Here comes the train, white face, Brewster green boiler, Pullman green tender, silver lettering — real sharp all around.

Flying green flags we see 604 arriving at Newtonville Mass. with 1st section of #27 New England State bound for Chicago. Train carried Deluxe reserved seat air conditioned coaches WESTBOUND ONLY. Date is June 17, 1940.

Norton D. Clark

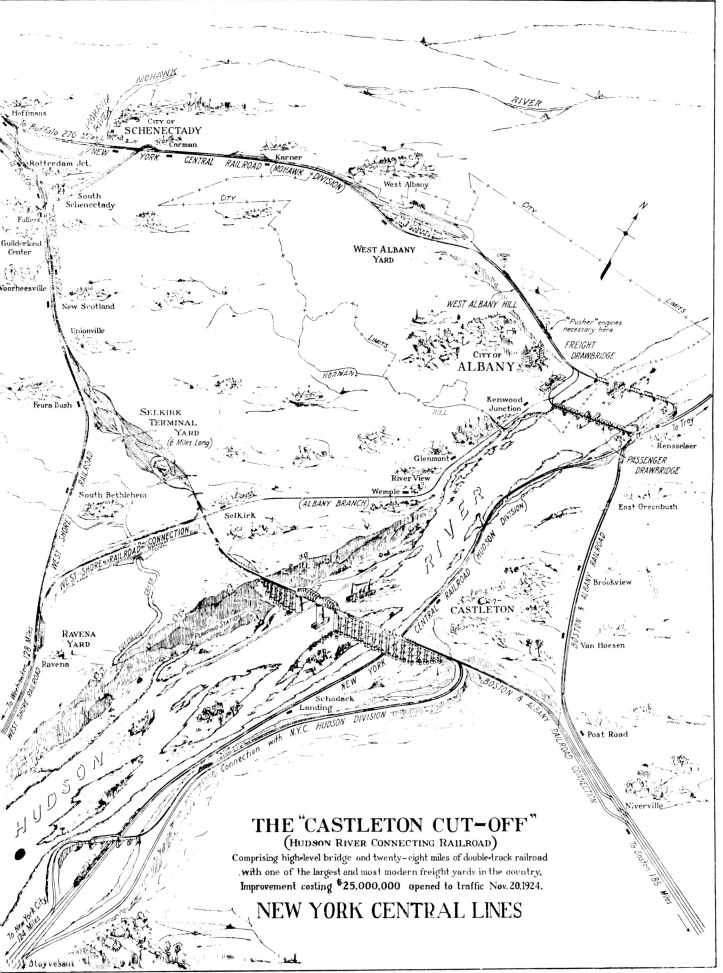

Line drawing that includes most of the main nerve center of the New York Central.

613 running on the main stem with what looks like Poughkeepsie Croton way freight at Cold Springs, N.Y. This is the only NYC Hudson we have ever seen with over fire jets (smoke consumers) of this type which, incidentally, don't seem to be working right now.

B&A #46 coming through North Grafton, Mass. Train has diner Pittsfield to Boston, sleepers from Cleveland, Toroto, Detroit and Buffalo, plus a lounge car from Albany — but no coaches.

Norton D. Clark

Norton D. Clark

September 15, 1928. Nearly brand new No. 600 with 20th Century Limited leaving Boston about 12:30 P.M.

12 car Wolverine (B&A #8) barrels by Allston, Mass. station and tower 10. Engineer has just finished waving to the kids in front.

Norton D. Clark

WOLVERINE

THE KNICKERBOCKER

Heavy Action in Twin Ledges, Middlefield, Mass. Train 49 The Knickerbocker, Boston — St. Louis. J2c 616 handles 8 cars unassisted. Usually a 1200 (2-8-2 Mike) would push from Chester to Washington. This is the toughest part of westbound climb.

The exhaust echoes, shattering back and forth between these hills, create a deafening continuous roar.

Robert A. Buck

Fireman's view from cab of A1c 2-8-4 Berkshire, we think. Big sand dome complicates identification. For sure though, oncoming power is J1b 609. Picture is real typical mid 1930, everything clean and neat and not a super highway or damned jet stream in sight.

MEET

Rail Photo Service

Ed Nowak - New York Central

Engineer's view from cab of K14 or K3 Pacific, we think. Rushing head on is B&A Hudson with Limited.

Norton D. Clark

One seldom found NYC Hudsons parked next to 4-4-0's or other Hudsons for that matter.
Above is 611 towering over New Haven's 1262 and below is New Haven's 1404 towering over 619. Both photos in Boston's South Station.
Also below, the cars on the far left aren't Erie "Stillwells" but ex-N.Y. Westchester and Boston.

Norton D. Clark

BOSTON

January 3, 1933, 613 on Century in South Station. All J2 Hudsons had Coffin closed type feedwater heaters. This heater is similar to the Elesco closed type except it wraps around inside the smoke box instead of protruding out the top or front. The closed heater is sort of a miniature boiler only we have steam heating water instead of fire heating water and creating steam.

Al Staufer collection

Complex shadows add to the confusion of a complex machine. 601 sports a hand-me-down J1 Hudson tender.

J2 POWER

607 battles up-grade eastbound with Train #6 at Worcester, Mass. Tender is J1.

Philip R. Hastings

...nson bar down in the corner, booster cut ...nd nothing but smoke and power as 615 ...s noon train to New York City out of Worester, Mass. January 2, 1939.

...on D. Clark

B&A Hudson No. 1 (600) on B&A train #40 "North Shore Limited", Chatham, New York, August 11, 1946.

Edward L. May

Norton D. Clark

Brand spanty new 608, just two months old and showing it, on the Boston section of the 20th Century, passing through Faneuil section of Brighton and heading west into the Newtons. October 13, 1930.
    Train is every bit as classy looking as main line #25. $9.60 extra fare to Chicago too.
    Put this back on the track, just the way she is here and our air traffic (highway too) congestion would be solved RIGHT NOW!

TWENTIETH CENTURY LIMITED

OHIO STATE LIMITED

#15 "Ohio State Limited" with Pullmans for Cincinnati, St. Louis, and the usual Albany coach, diner, lounge. Shown here on one of the few short straightaways on the B&A where they took advantage by "pouring the coals" to her. Southville, Mass., November 4, 1938.
    Even with her damned square sand box and droopy cab, 616 looks good.

Norton D. Clark

600 (as built and straight cab) passing Tower 6 at Huntington Ave., Boston with the Wolverine on May 20, 1934 about 4:30 P.M. D.S.T. In the consist are diner, and coach to Albany, two Chicago and one Detroit sleepers.

606 westbound on Track 3 with #15 "Ohio State Limited". Normally this track is used by suburban locals but you'll note the work extra dropping ties for rebuilding Track #1.

OHIO STATE LIMITE

Norton D. Clark

Norton D. Clark

Lots going here. Hudson 606 helping two diesels (Alco PA1's 4200's 2000 HP class DPA-2) handle 17 car New England State Ltd. by Newton, Mass. November 4, 1949. Cars are all stainless steel. Also note 300 series tank loco coming in with a Boston commuter run.

NEW ENGLAND STATE

611 as seen from Tower #6 pulling the Boston section of the "Century" into Huntington Ave. Station. December 26, 1932.
Note contrast of cane seat suburban coaches left and plush Century Pullmans right.

Norton D. Clark

J3 SUPER HU

SONS

William A. Raia collection

The first impact of the great depression was making itself felt as the J1 fleet was being built. On many other railroads, the orders would have been reduced or cancelled, but the still wealthy Central took delivery on all ordered J1 and J2 Hudsons. There they were with the finest stable of runners known to man when the bottom fell out of the passenger market. They were utilized with the usual priorities of best engines taking the best trains. Many a lesser train that rated no more than a K3 Pacific was wheeled along with THOROUGHBREDS. Service and on-time performance must have been fantastic on all Lines during the early "thirties."

So in 1935 the New York Central had, in essence, light passenger demands and more Hudsons than it could shake a stick at. So what did it do? It ordered 50 super Hudsons which, to the best of our knowledge, was the largest single order for steam locomotives at the very depth of the depression.

J3 super Hudson at its massive best rolling into Chicago on a clear day in February, 1946.

Streamlined 5450 blew up at Canastota, N.Y. on eastbound Century September 7, 1943. Loco is seen here with Selkirk front end (and new boiler) received at West Albany September 23, 1944.

Drivers and front of first J3 Hudson.   New York Central

It sounds totally illogical, but let's analyze the facts. True, they had no immediate need for passenger flyers but they did need locomotives at the other end of the scale. They were still running 25 year old 4-6-2's. So when you need more power, overall, you obviously don't order obsolete classes; you order "top of the line" stuff and bump down the line accordingly. Your newest Hudsons bump older Hudsons, older Hudsons the late Pacifics, and so on and so on down the line till you reach the point when you begin pulling ancients from service and retiring them.

Other factors enter in. First, the Central could no more finance this deal (total cost over 12 million including new passenger cars) than I could buy the Brooklyn Bridge. Money, or backing, had to come from somewhere. That somewhere was a certain tall "co-signer" who is noted for his generosity and colorful red, white, and blue outfit — including hat. Actual cash or loan was laid on them by some big New York bank (part by Irving Trust Company), but standing in the wing with guarantee was the Reconstruction Finance Corporation. I think they called it "pump priming", theory being that if you pump some financial aid here, it works its way through many — many hands resulting in stimulating many areas other than the source which was in this case— locomotive builder.

The streamliners were coming and Central knew it. They had already streamlined a Hudson (5344), but the real pacesetters and creators of the fad were blown in from prevailing westerly winds in the form of Burlington's "Zephyrs" and Union Pacific's "Train of Tomorrow." When U.P.'s "Streamliner" was displayed at Grand Central Terminal, the fervor and interest did not go unnoticed by President Williamson and his executive V.P. Raymond Starbuck.

Pullman was building new smooth sided, round roof, big windowed sleepers that would eventually replace the standard clerestory roof heavyweights. Management was impressed. Wouldn't a string of those in two tone gray or green look great on the Century? This new concept in trains would certainly merit an increase in speed. It was to be. But what could improve on the J1e Hudson?

There was never any question about it — the Hudson was destined to succeed itself. As stated in a previous chapter, the J1 was a locomotive ahead of its time. Their time had come. Now was the chance to develop the type to the ultimate. Between the building of 5344 and the first J3 (5405) the Hudson was in some phase of advance planning.

With a prototype fleet of 205 J1's for starters, you ought to build yourself quite a machine. They did.

With the possible exception of Pennsy, we know of no road that did so much design engineering. The Central did most of the planning on the new J3's. Actually, we're surprised they didn't go up to Schenectady and build it themselves.

What was this super engine like, anyway? Basically, it was very similar to the last J1e's, but literally packed with every available gadget and design feature — to squeeze out every ounce of power with no appreciable change in weight. There's no other way to put it. It was simply a "super-sophisticate machine." We think it was so "much" that perhaps a larger locomotive with different wheel arrangement would have been better, but more on that later. Basic changes incorporated in the J3's not found in J1's were: combustion chamber; all roller bearing wheels; conical boiler; higher pressure and smaller cylinders.

158

New York Central

Two men we wish we could identify for you. Silver graphite for special occasions and special engines only.

Even rear of tender is good looking. Also, we like the serif type lettering style. Lower sheet metal is deflector from scooping water.

New York Central

SPECIFICATIONS

	J3a	J1e
Cylinders	22½ x 29"	25 x 2
Drivers	79"	79"
Boiler Pressure	†275 lbs.	225 lb
*Engine Weight	360,000	352,00
Engine Weight Streamlined	365,000	— —
Tractive Force (with booster)	53,900	53,26
Grate Area	82 sq. ft.	81.5 sq.
Total Heating Surface	4,187 sq. ft.	4,480 sq.
Horsepower	4,725 @ 75 m.p.h.	3,900 @
Tender Capacity Coal	30 tons	28 ton
Tender Capacity Water	14,000 gals.	14,000 ga

† later reduced to 265 lbs.
*engine weight **varied**

MECHANICAL FEATURES

5405 to 5454, Schenectady Sept. 1937 to April 1938
Cost:

5405-5444	$120,000.00 each
5445-5449	132,000.00 each
5450-5454	139,000.00 each

Nickel Steel Conical Boiler Shell
    91" at largst ring and 80⅝ smallest (J1e - 87⅝ and 82½)

Combustion Chamber 43" long

Tube Length 19' (J1e 20'6")

Brick Arch in Firebox Supported on 4 Water Tubes

Type E Superheater

Enlarged Steam and Exhaust Passages

Cast Steel Frame with Integral Cylinders

Drivers — Scullin Double Disc and Commonwealth Boxpok

Roller Bearings on all Wheels Engine and Tender
    Side and main rods solids except 5450-5454 Timken

Reverse Cylinder — Located on main frame instead of usual right side

Multiple Front End Throttle

Automatic Train Control

C-2 Booster (Some with exhaust in tender, others exhaust ahead of main stack)

HT Stoker

Elesco Feedwater Heater

Baker Valve Gear

Loco Valve Pilot

Aluminum cab and running boards on 40 engines including the 10 Streamlined

Larger sand dome than J1

All tenders had water scoops and coal pushers

Tight-lock couplers   Streamlined tenders

Lightweight alloy steel, piston and rod assembly.

New York Central

Appears to be President Williamson in cab. Looks like VP Starbuck standing in gangway.

Obviously, the impact of improvements on the J3 was in the boiler and firebox. This increased weight by 15,800 lbs., but was mostly offset by trimming weight wherever possible elsewhere (cab, rods, etc.). Deep within the boiler lie the very heart of the J3 Hudson. It was the combustion chamber, which could be likened to the superheater in that you literally get something for nothing. By merely leaving a space for gasses to burn more completely ahead of the firebox you squeeze more from an otherwise identical boiler. Stay bolt leakage presents service difficulties, and you lose heating surface with shorter tubes but overall heat exchange is increased enormously. Almost all road locomotives from the early 20's on had them. Only notable exception we know of were the J1 Hudsons. In their design it was reasoned that enormous grate area and longer tubes would produce sufficient steam. It did. But when you set forth to build a super engine it is the most logical improvement.

The J3 boiler was shaped differently from the J1's being fatter at the largest ring and skinnier at the smokebox. Visually, this was not too apparent as the boiler was practically flat on top. Fattest shell was rolled so the bulge was to the sides and bottom.

Combustion chamber meant shorter tubes which in turn meant less smokebox area. No matter how much steam your boiler can generate, it isn't worth a hoot if it can't be delivered to the cylinders in corresponding ratio. And that's a dickens of a problem in a confined space. Problem was solved in Central's usual approach, tests, tests, tests, and more tests. A myriad of arrangements were tried until the best passage capacity and design were found. They were ultimately much larger than those in the J1's.

Boiler pressure was raised from 225 lbs. (J1) to 275 lbs., which permitted cylinder dimensions to be altered from 25 x 28″ to 22½ x 29″. Even with this smaller diameter and longer stroke the original J3 developed too much thrust or kick. So much so that they were creating excessive stresses (even bending) in the main rods. Rather than redesign the rods they lowered steam pressure 10 lbs. to 265 and that eliminated the problem.

The pursuit of weight reduction was almost fanatical. More weight on drivers was desirable, but not too much. When all the aluminum and nickel steel dust settled the increase of weight on drivers was a mere 1,400 lbs. over the latest J1's. Lighter rods meant lighter counter weights, thus relieving the devastating hammer blow to rails that was second nature to the steam animal.

There was a very startling break in precedence with this order of 50 locomotives. The entire order was placed — WHAM — just like that. NO I — YES — NO, or sample locomotive; just a flat out order. Reason: Central needed passenger locomotives and the J3 just had to be a little better than the latest J1e.

Soon after completion 5408 was pulled from service and put through exhaustive tests on the Mohawk division with trains weighing from 766 tons to 1,609 tons.

161

PERFORMANCE OF J3 CLASS LOCOMOTIVE COMPARED WITH PREVIOUSLY TESTED J1

	Maximum Power		Improvement,
	J-1	J-3	J-3 per cent
Tractive effort with booster, lb.	55100	55000	— — —
Main-engine tractive effort, lb.	45400	45000	— — —
Main-engine drawbar pull, lb.	41300	41500	— — —
Cylinder Horsepower	3900	4725	21.1
	at 67 m.p.h.	at 75 m.p.h.	11.9
Cylinder horsepower per pair of driving wheels	1300	1575	21.1
Drawbar horsepower	3240	3880	19.75
	at 58 m.p.h.	at 65 m.p.h.	12.1
	Average performance division run of 140 miles		
Number of cars and weight in tons	18-1244	18-1253	
Working speed, m.p.h.	55	59	
Firing rate, dry coal per hour, lb.	6940	6419	
Water delivered to boiler per hour, lb.	57200	54900	
Evaporation per pound of dry coal, lb.	8.24	8.32	1.0
Combined efficiency; boiler, feedwater heater, and superheater, per cent	74.6	76.3	2.3
Steam per indicated horsepower-hour, lb.			
Cylinders only	15.44	14.76	4.4
Including auxiliaries	17.28	16.89	2.3
Dry coal per indicated horsepower-hour, lb.			
Cylinders only	1.94	1.84	5.15
Including auxiliaries	2.10	2.03	3.3
Coal fired per car mile, lb.	7.03	6.21	11.7
Weight per indicated horsepower, lb.	90	76	15.5

Preceding page shows 5405 under steam for the first time. Above, the officials look 'er over and by cripes, I wish I could jump in the picture and join them. Looks like Starbuck walking past port cylinder.

We report these tests as a matter of duty to complete the full Hudson story but we feel the results quite mysterious and even inconclusive. The comparisons are with a previously tested J1. This is perfectly fine, but which one? Was it the latest J1e or an earlier model. Increased drawbar horsepower of almost 20% is most impressive.

What really matters is what they did out on the road. The J1's were good, the J3's a little better. A little better than "great" is most adequate. There was no way to squeeze one more ounce of power from the 4-6-4 without just building a much larger locomotive. They have to be rated "A+" for performance and availability, running almost 20,000 miles a month and going over one quarter million miles between classified repairs.

When the J3's were ordered, there was no "flyer" emergency, but gathering storm clouds in the east soon altered that. World War II ended the depression and rail traffic in America was to rise to its greatest and probably never to be equaled height. Central was ready and delivered. Whatever was designed into the J3's had full opportunity to express itself in millions upon millions of miles.

Let us stray overseas for a comparison of events. The original exponent of superhighways was Adolph Hitler. In the 30's his Autobahns were crisscrossing the Fatherland while German railroads were left relatively untouched. As the war ground on it became all too apparent which mode of transportation could deliver when the chips were down. Unlikely as it may seem, railroads are much more flexible. One well placed bomb on a superhighway in the winter or spring, and you have an instant sea of mud. Same bomb on a track gives you the same sea of mud, but you can lay new track right over that mud and keep running trains. It's a matter of weight distribution and flexibility of materials. America was spared that horror but was faced with the movement of all materials over its 3000 mile breadth.

Starting in 1943, every single J3 had its Elesco feedwater replaced with the Worthington SA's. This type heater is "live" with exhaust steam coming in direct contact with the cold water, while the Elesco's heat was transferred through tubes. The Worthington heater was far more efficient, easier to maintain and had almost limitless capacity. After improvement in their ability to separate lubricants and impurities from the exhaust steam they became the dominant heater used on U.S. railroads.

The frame mounted reversing gears were moved to conventional location below right side air tank as cylinder repairs were made. One of the rules governing steam locomotive practices in America was "ease of maintenance takes precedence over delicate refinements." Just the opposite was true in Europe. It all boils down to this: we are a big land, move heavy stuff far and fast, and pay our men high wages. It's not good economics to horse around.

All 50 J3's, including the streamliners, were eventually fitted with the PT centipede tenders.

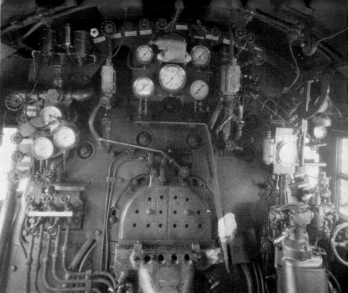

Beautiful serif lettering is "Printer's Roman" as near as we can tell. All changed to san serif modern around 1940. Note inductor and receiver for ATC, lower right.

Backhead of 5405. Five valves, lower left, are fireman's stoker adjustments for regulating even fire. Row of valves near cab roof go to turret and control steam heat, feedwater pump heat, coal pushers, etc.

Average cost for PT tender was about $55,000.00 and most were built by Lima Locomotive Works. They carried enough coal for most Hudson runs and were able to pick up water at 80 m.p.h. Preliminary studies were made for a super tender with coal capacity of 75 tons (enough for the N.Y. - Chicago run) but were discarded since coaling facilities were needed for all other freight power anyway. The very fine displaced J3 tenders were fitted to other Hudsons, K5 Pacifics, 2-8-2 Mikados, and L2 Mohawks. The fact that all were built alike paid off in these big tender swap years.

The whole realm of J3 drivers is absolutely baffling and beyond our best logical reasoning. Supposedly half were fitted with Boxpok and half Scullin Disc, though our photos seem to indicate a 2/3 ratio favoring the Boxpok. The ten streamlined were divided equally, 5445-5449 Boxpok and 5450-5454 disc. The mystery lies in the way and frequency these drivers were exchanged. We have cases where a given engine was built new with Boxpok, almost immediately had them replaced with disc, then had Boxpok appear again, maybe this time with a Baldwin disc main driver thrown in for good luck. This is not an isolated case. It kept happening right to the end. The only continuity we can detect is that no matter what combination was used the 1st and 3rd drivers were alike (well, almost always).

We will attempt a meager explanation. War time demands were severe and unyielding. When a J3 came into Collinwood, Beech Grove, or West Albany for class repairs, they simply put on drivers that were ready to go. Only flaw in that theory is they were doing it long before the war started. Maybe demand for J3's was just always that great. There was, however, some attempt to have "like" drivers on the streamlined engines.

We can never accuse the Central of being deficient in the area of testing. Hardly ! On the contrary, one could more justly accuse them of doing all tests for all builders and all roads. In 1937 they initiated a series of stationary boiler front end arrangements at Selkirk to determine the best steam and exhaust passage size and design. The results were surprisingly successful, with increased evaporation rate upwards of 10%. Ultimately over 500 NYC engines were either built or rebuilt to the new standards.

After streamling was removed 5447, 5450*, 5451 and 5453 had boiler fronts rebuilt in the flat (L4 Mohawk) front style. Still testing, testing, testing.

Most, maybe all, booster engines were removed and the J3's missed them just as much as the J1's did. We were in the era of four coupled dual purpose locomotives. No time here to fool around with complex boosters.

The Hudson had had its day. Summing up briefly: The J3's were relatively small by modern motive power standards. They were perpetually worked to the upper limits of their capacity. Maybe, just maybe, it would have been wiser to build bigger engines and work them easier. Such designs were available in 1936. But we speak from the vantage point of History and I'm certain that if Paul Kiefer had been capable of that magic, he would have done many things differently.

The J3's were the last Hudsons built for the New York Central System.

*5450 got back original front end later.

New York Central

Timken roller bearings on engine and SKF on Commonwealth built tender trucks. Pyle turbo generator (top) could generate enough electricity for a country town but was only for loco and tender needs.

Elesco cold water pump (lower left) was mounted below tender water level and was the most often used feed system.

J3 5405
THOROUGHBRED
1937

Schenectady, September, 1937. Here sits the first super Hudson. Major changes between 5405 and its J1 predecessor were boiler and cylinder size, addition of combustion chamber, roller bearings all wheels engine and tender (not side rods) and Boxpok drivers (some had disc).

First major change to J3's was to move reverse cylinder from between frame to conventional position below air tank right side. Object below air tank on 5405 is Locomotive Valve Pilot.

Greatest flaw was the selection of the Elesco feedwater heater. All 50 J3's had their Elesco heaters replaced with the much more efficient Worthington open type.

All 50 J3's eventually received PT centipede tenders.

As usual these "as built" photographs show the engine at its absolute best in appearance. Neat and trim. No way can the application of later hardware do anything but clutter things up.

5405 in Harmon, June 5, 1949 and hardly in original livery. Drivers are now Scullin disc, feedwater heater and tender replaced, and outside reverse cylinder.

Edward L. May

No. 5405

OHIO STATE LIMITED

168-169
5405 scorching the ballast by Manitou, N.Y. with the Ohio State Limited on June 16, 1940. Bear Mountain bridge in background.
Pretty much as built except beautiful serif lettering has given way to san serif modern Two of the eleven cars are streamlined two tone gray.

Edward L. May

Al Staufer   5405 in Collinwood, Ohio, 1954 with J1 5389. Center driver is back to original Boxpok and 1st and 3rd are Union Steel Castings, Web-Spoke type.

Left side of 5408 after installation of Worthington feedwater heater. In this system, the tender water is pumped (centrifugal, near trailing truck) directly to the heater (top of boiler front) then is fed to the boiler by a hot water pump (above cylinder).

Howard W. Rosentreter

Wilson Jones

THE

COMMODORE VANDERBILT

5406 on Train #37 "Advance Commodore Vanderbilt", Beacon, N.Y. August 9, 1941. No. 37 is new train about this time though 37 is old "Advance Century's" number. This train (Advance Commodore) later changed to #65.

Real hot shot, no passengers on this baby except Pullman passengers bound from New York to Englewood or Chicago. No Toledo, No Elkhart, No sir!

Consist is:
- 2 — 6 double bedroom buffet lounge
- 2 — 18 roomettes
- 1 — 10 roomette, 5 double bedroom
- 1 — 4 compartment, 4 bedroom, 2 drawing room
- 1 — 13 double bedroom
- 1 — 14 section
- 1 — Diner
- 1 — Baggage

5409 and L4 Mohawk at Linndale, Ohio (suburb of Cleveland).

Herb Harwood

171

5410 at Harmon, N.Y. December 5, 1937. Absolutely mint spanking brand new with not one revenue mile on her. The way Alco built them.

Edward L. May

THE PACEMAKER

5411 with 12 car #1 "The Pacemaker" at Oscawana, N.Y. April, 1946. Beautiful trac beautiful train.

Edward L. May

Harmon, N.Y. August 3, 1946. Surprisingly, 5413 still retains the inside reverse gear and Elesco feedwater heater. Lord knows what her original drivers were but now they are Boxpok with Disc main. Tender is replaced with Lima built P.T.

Examine closely and note how many piping changes there are compared to 5410 preceding page.

Edward L. May

Bob Lorenz

Engineer Herman Sabroske on "Fifth Avenue Special" by Vickers tower east of Toledo, Ohio.

There is a slight tremble throughout this photograph caused by both speed and massive loco shaking everything in sight.

Seventeen year old J3a at White Pigeon, Michigan. There's no question at all that the PT tenders were just too big and hulky for the New York Central Hudson type locomotive. This almost identical tender looks just great on the S class 4-8-4 Niagaras.

Edward L. May

Only application of dual sealed beam headlights on a Hudson. When this photo was taken (March 30, 1948) they were already applied to all the 4-8-4's so this was obviously an experiment that didn't merit duplication.

Also excellent view of Worthington feedwater heater.

Ed Nowak - New York Central

174

Backing down from 63rd St. to La Salle St. Station. W. H. N. Rossiter

PT TENDER DATA

	Gallons	Tons	Wt. Empty	Wt. Loaded	Used on
PT1	17,500	43	169,300	401,100	J1c, J3a
PT2	21,000	25	155,700	380,700	J1 5401
PT3	18,000	46	178,000	420,000	J1b, J1c, J3a
PT4	18,000	46	178,000	420,000	J1's, J3's, S1b
PT5	18,000	46	178,000	420,000	all S class and J3a

The PT tenders were big, just 2' shorter than the engine and 30 tons heavier when fully loaded.

Was it worth the effort to haul around the equivalent of an extra heavyweight Pullman? Yes.

Beech Grove, March 1943. First P.T. tender built for a Hudson. Ed Nowak - New York Central

Edward L. May

There is nothing that we are aware of that sets Hudson 5418 apart or any different from any other of the 50 J3 super Hudsons.

What does make 5418 just a bit special is that we happen to have five photographs of her at strategic stages of her existence (one following page).

Above, 5418 at Englewood, Ill., December 2, 1937. Here she sits "as built" — Boxpok drivers — serif lettering — still a faint whiff of the smell of new paint about her.

5418

Al Staufer collection

5418 in about late 1940. Note disc wheels.

Maybe we "stew" and make more of the driver switching than it's really worth. Maybe Central just bought all the drivers it could get in these early days of WW II shortages. These disc, Boxpok, and Web Spoke were primarily used on J3 Hudsons with their relatively light side rods.

Charles H. Kerrigan

5418 with eastbound "Pacemaker", La Salle St Station, Chicago, August, 1947. We now have Worthington feedwater heater, PT tank, 3rd driver disc and 1st and main Boxpok.

J3 5418

5418 at Englewood, July, 1952. Main driver is Boxpok and 1st and 3rd Web-Spoke.

Engineer is talking to left side fire box with a king sized monkey wrench.

W. H. N. Rossiter

Edward L. May

Above: 5420 at Peekskill, July 20, 1941 with #67 Commodore Vanderbilt. 39 Chevy in background is Ed May's.
   Above right: Bitter cold, January 29, 1940, 5420 on name train. Note fierce booster exhaust and Pennsy's great "Broadway" to left.
Right: 5418 again, December 16, 1939 with what appears to be eastbound "Commodore" at Englewood.

THE COMMODORE VANDERBILT

Al Staufer collection

Al Staufer collection

J3

Rail Photo Service

"Albany Express" rips through rocky ridges at Peekskill, New York. Could be maiden trip for 5422 as she appears brand new.

Edward L. May

Another one of these "fresh from the builders" gems. Harmon, New York, December 5, 1937. Those shiny aluminum cylinder covers look great.

Over two decades and three million miles later, 5423 has lost a bit of lustre — to say the least: pound for pound there is more new iron than original in 5423.
    Let us count the ways: (1) new tender (2) booster gone (3) different feedwater heater system (4) different drivers (5) different stack and inner steam pipes. And scads more we can't even see or don't know about.

CLEVELAND

5424 exudes a brutish charm in this "as built" photo. Things are sort of massive and slab-like, all except the relatively delicate boiler front. We like it. Overhead wires are for Cleveland terminal electrics and location is Linndale, Ohio on Cleveland's west side.

P.S.: Forgive the cropped off pilot. Too many zealous fans get carried away by the blow-up thrill in the dark room.

Glenn Monhart collection

Here's 5424, 11 years old at Chicago on May 23, 1948. Obviously and always the as built versions were supreme in appearance. Why? Because they were designed with that factor totally in mind. Seldom can tack-on hardware enhance over-all appeal.

Jack McGroarty

The three main shops on the New York Central capable of class repairs were Collinwood, West Albany and Beech Grove. 5427 is on the Collinwood turntable.

Forgive my personal reflection, but many a time I wandered through this house by the looming faces of Central's power from switchers to the largest passengers. The stillness was broken by the occasional throbs of the forward air pumps, letting you know they were quite alive. The Niagaras were the most massive but nothing struck one more severely than the leaning brow of the 2700 Mohawks.

CHICAGO

5425 under coal chutes at 63rd St. roundhouse — Chicago.

W. H. N. Rossiter

"As built" in July 3, 1938. Edward L. May

EMPIRE STATE EXPRESS

5426 was one of the more famous Hudsons because of the Empire State Express streamlining (see poster page 8).

"Empire" shroud was removed November 4, 1950 at Collinwood. 5426 still handles the "Empire State Express" and quite well too.

Westbound at Buchanan, New York. The smoke looks most dramatic but train is only doing about 40 mph. The really high speed smoke lays back there much lower to the engine.

R. P. Zits

184

Edward L. May — The moving outboard of the power reverse necessitated moving the air tank up, thus breaking up the neat straight running board.

EXPRESS

Robert A. Whitbeck

When its below zero out there you pray your shutter clicks OK, cause if it does you've got yourself a picture.
With steam oozing from every portal 5436 rushes a westbound mail and express at Rome, New York.

Ed Nowak - New York Central

5433 all painted and cleaned up waiting to be towed into Grand Central Terminal for the 300th anniversary of New York City, September 10, 1953.
No smoke allowed in clean "fun city" you know.

Bob Lorenz

Poughkeepsie, New York. Headed west standing in station on track #1.
The mighty NEW YORK CENTRAL!

LAKE SHORE LIMITED

Everything is pretty well right in this picture. Engine is absolutely as built, straight running board, original tender and even a bit of shine to the aluminum hand rails and cylinder covers.

Date is August 9, 1941 and 5435 heads the "Lake Shore Limited" #22 on track #2 towards New York City.

Train is ready to enter Breakneck Tunnel. Note clean ballast and Hudson river on left.

Wilson Jones

Chicago, September, 1947. Paul Strayer, who took this photo said "burly engineer on a heavy brutish designed engine". When compared to the sleek J1, we agree.

rd L. May

e first few surges of exhaust from a locomotive
t starts a heavy load are difficult to describe be-
e they must be felt as much as seen. 5437 with
No. 67 at Harmon. As train photos go — Not
not bad at all.

No matter how fast it looks, in 1941 you slowed to 50 mph to take water on the fly.
   Train is the first #38 "Missourian" which was always late. Not, however, due to the efforts of the J3a Hudson.
   Tivoli, New York, August 30, 1941.

Edward L. May

5437 races up the Hudson with the 2nd #67 "Commodore Vanderbilt". Note the low sun angle. Remember that New York City is on the eastern edge of the eastern time zone. Actually, daylight saving time had its start in the populous east. It darned sure isn't needed in Ohio, which is one full daylight hour west.

Edward L. May

5442 has just been delivered from Schenectady and waits here at Harmon for early voyage, December 5, 1937.

The most massive of them all, a J3 with disc drivers, PT tender and Selkirk front end.

De-streamlined 5452 still had Elesco heater in 1946.

J3

Harold Stirton collection

Jack McGroarty, an old friend, clerked at both Linndale and Collinwood, so was directly associated with the day to day problems of locomotives that the rest of us are unaware of. We quote some of his random thoughts on Hudsons in general, not just the J3's.

"Each loco was a custom built machine. After acceptance tests it belonged to the road. In each major backshop the equipment is there to build — rebuild — replace all parts except for drivers, air brake parts, wheels, which were purchased outside. A new fire box was made in the backshop, such as Collinwood, Beech Grove, West Albany. Flues were purchased but cut and fit in place. New cast engine beds were purchased but cast to specs from RR Co., i.e., a custom job. Tenders were built, altered, rebuilt in kind, changed to stoker engine equipped and stoker screw only. Stokers were purchased from firebox distributor, plates were custom made and purchased but always repaired or replaced by the roundhouse as a running repair. Front ends were made by the RR Co.

Netting was made, replaced, repaired, removed and changed. Exhaust nozzles likewise. Pilots on new engines were purchased and replacements were purchased. Bells were purchased, domes fabricated. Springs were built in backshops and replaced in roundhouses. Number plates were cast at backshops. Valve gear was purchased but all repairs including making new parts done in roundhouses. All piping was done in roundhouses, even changes done as running repair. Each roundhouse had a complete machine shop to make bearings, etc. and a foundry to make castings, etc.

In backshop, boiler firebox back heads were hammered out in a die on the floor by men with sledge hammers, smoke box fronts also — hard to believe but true!

To repair any engine the roundhouse had a drop table to remove drivers from engines. These were sent to the backshop to be cut and have driving boxes repaired or serviced and shipped back to roundhouse and installed. Beech Grove was the only backshop that could table the drivers of a 6000. Many engines had test equipment of all kinds on them — all classes. Parts that were on test from parts manufacturers.

We made everything for the engine, even a broken rod was forged and machined at the backshop. Bearing blocks were machined and fitted with Prussian Blue and installed. Tires were replaced in roundhouse but not often — this was backshop work. All parts were welded, brazed, etc. by our own people.

The B4 Hudsons were always clean — cleaner than the Mainline engines — usually they only ran 2 divisions — Linndale to Indianapolis or Linndale to Cincinnati.

The 5344 had new cylinders and saddle, too. So the cylinders and saddle were welded to the frame. The engine would run hot on the main pin on the fireman's side. It was so hot when it would come in from Toledo that you could fry an egg on the pin. She was just a little out of tram on that side because the cylinder saddle would shift slightly. But at million mile inspection the Timken bearings showed no visible wear.

Clerking at Linndale and making out work reports from crews at the end of runs, I found that the Hudsons gave very little trouble. They were many years ahead of their time for the job and over-engineered. The most common complaints were:
1. Gauges not working.
2. Broken driver springs or cocked in saddle.
3. Front end netting plugged with the dirt burned as passenger coal. (There were two kinds — passenger and freight.)
4. Broken driver spokes (welded at roundhouse).
5. Chafing block — or buffer casting between engine and tank would loosen up. Springs would loosen tension and wouldn't hold and tender would pound against engine on each revolution.
6. Loose driving box wedges would cause surging on each piston stroke and it felt like the frame was working but the Hudsons had cast beds by 1950.
7. Air leaks — found by machinist inspection.
8. Steam leaks — mostly piston packing.
9. Stiff throttles — linkage.
10. Hard riding — Hard riders were few but those that rode hard were built that way. By 1950 these engines had been torn down to the bare frame 5 or 6 times on 5-Year overhauls, and hard riding was never cured.

I can't recall any serious problems with tenders. They just seemed to come along for the ride. I don't know of any rhyme or reason to the PT tank program — it seemed that most through engines had them but this was not a fast rule. The J3's had the blow down piped to the rear of the tank with a red sign stating this stenciled on the back of the tank. All air reservoirs were tested every year by an air man — he used a small sledge hammer, and pounded on every square inch of the reservoir. This was then hydrotested - This is the information stenciled on the tank, last test etc. This was still the cast iron age. Hard to believe." Jack got this quote from an old hostler nick-named "Stage Coach".

"All the J1's and J3's had a personality and they were all individuals. We all had our favorite girl. And girls they were — some were just nice girls, some were whores and you had to beat them every mile of track, and some were prima donnas and would only perform for certain men, (or in my case at the time boys) and some were Queens and would let you know that they were — you fired light and kept the water in the center of the glass and they would walk out of town with a train which would have a sister on her knees. The 5450 was one of those Queens, one didn't beat her, she ran like a deer at short cut off. All of the crews knew them for their colors after 15 or 25 years on the road."

Bob Lorenz

EMD F7's bulk-up pretty good but not enough to diminish the size of a J3 with a PT tank.

Companion photo to above. Toledo, Ohio.

Bob Lorenz

LAKE SHORE LIMITED

Gerald M. Frank

When you speed over a fresh dusting of snow the aerodynamics are such that the entire train is immediately enveloped in a white mass.

Jack McGroarty collection

Not an uncommon sight in the early 50's. Train is eastbound through Vermilion, Ohio, and either they are balancing power or Fairbanks-Morse steam generator broke down.

Empire State Express approaching tunnel at Oscawana, Track #1. Thick winter h along the Hudson River.

Ed Nowak - New York Centra

CLEVELAND

5447 arriving Cleveland's lakefront with mail and express from Chicago. Notice PT tender coal pile. Car in foreground is Kaiser and second is brand new 54 Chevy.

Al Staufer

Ed Nowak - New York Central

Eastward bound on the Mohawk Division.

STREAMLIN

ING

Edward L. May

It had to follow that when man invented a machine that would fly, it would inevitably become the pacesetter for all other things. To make the machine work better it was soon found that as with God's birds, smooth rounded surfaces worked better. The "aeroplane" became the thing. Streamlining was here and just about every commercial product from the mid-twenties on was affected. Airflow mattered. It was a new direction a designer could hang his hat on. First to feel the effects were automobiles, and eventually all succumbed, even buildings. Least likely candidate for this new fad was the very utilitarian steam locomotive. But it had to happen and it happened first on the New York Central.

Obvious class selection would be J1 Hudson and obvious locomotive would be one of the last two built (actually the last), No. 5344. Streamlining was a rather simple sheet metal shroud covering up most of the engine and tender. It really didn't look too bad. For a detailed account of this engine, see chapter titled "The Most Famous Hudson".

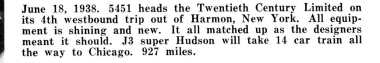

June 18, 1938. 5451 heads the Twentieth Century Limited on its 4th westbound trip out of Harmon, New York. All equipment is shining and new. It all matched up as the designers meant it should. J3 super Hudson will take 14 car train all the way to Chicago. 927 miles.

Central New York Chapter NR.

"Commodore Vanderbilt" (5344), New York Central's first streamlined engine passes next to conventional mate, 5310, near the old station at Franklin Street in Syracuse, New York. December, 1934.

Steam locomotives didn't adapt to streamlining very well because of the very way they were built and designed. Everything on them just "hung out there" for easy access, maintenance and repairs. Wrapping the whole thing in a piece of tin just had to be bad news to the roundhouse crews and not the least, the effects on air cooling of the valve motion parts.

5344, now named Commodore Vanderbilt, was the first of a streamlined craze that swept American railroads lasting almost two decades. Many railroads were rushing to complete new colorful trains and locomotives. A dimension of realism was added by Pullman's new streamlined cars that were most adaptable to lively colors.

New York Central's first all new train was to be its World renowned "Twentieth Century Limited". Exterior car shape was standard Pullman streamlined. All else was designed by 34-year-old Henry Dreyfuss, considered by most to be the most brilliant — prolific — industrial designer — EVER. His name was not a household word but almost every American has used his creation. A partial list of his works would be: Fly Swatters; Potatoe Peelers; Razors; Pens; Clocks; Door Knobs; Faucets; Fire Extinguishers; Typewriters; Cameras; Vacuum Cleaners; Radios; Television Sets; Air Conditioners; Refrigerators; Tractors; Dial Princess and Push Button Telephones; Interiors of the 707 Jetliner; and Ocean Liners "Constitution" and "Independence"; and the 1938 Twentieth Century Limited.

Assisting Dreyfuss were the engineers of Pullman Standard Car Company, New York Central and Alco. Entire consist facing the team was 62 passenger cars and 10 locomotives. Task was to create the most distinguished, luxurious train known to man. Basic limitations were the exterior shapes of the locomotives and cars.

The previous approach to steam locomotive streamlining was to cover the entire engine and tender with a shroud, like hiding the engine under a cover. Dreyfuss chose to utilize the basic form by wrapping the sheet metal as tightly as possible to engine and tender with all running gear and vital parts exposed. Domes were enclosed in a continuous contour that met the fin covered bullet nose at the boiler front. Tender had lower sheet metal skirts to conform with the shape of the Pullman cars which gave the over-all train a "unit" look sort of like a continuous piece of extruded aluminum. Speaking of aluminum, much was used in the Streamlined Hudsons to reduce weight.

A rather startling feature and departure from functionalism was the 3½ foot extension of the tender. The J3 Hudson tender is relatively short (about 40′) and we suspect Dreyfuss simply added the empty length for looks. Actually the streamlined tenders were almost 2′ shorter but about 1′ longer with extended shroud.

Perhaps the most important decision facing the design team was color. Dignified color was a must for the Twentieth Century Limited but more importantly, color selection would be a style setter on the New York Central for years to come. We don't know "who" was for "what" color but final selection was narrowed down to shades of green or gray. It was resolved in the usual manner of official viewings of painted models. It was no contest. The "Grays" had the class and so it was. The cars for the Twentieth Century Limited had black roofs, medium gray sides with blue edged dark gray bands running through the windows. Thin silver stripes ran at the roof and floorlines and two broader silver stripes through the dark gray and on the tender sides. Separating all colors were thin black lines. Engine and tender were same medium grey of cars except that driving wheels and front cowl fin were painted a satin aluminum. Rods, cylinder and valve covers were natural metal.

There it stood with 13 cars, 1,194 feet long and weight over 1,070 tons. Weight was about one-third (⅓) less than previous standard equipment.

Harmon, New York, Summer, 1936. Central's second (and least successful) streamlining efforts were applied to two K5 Pacifics, 4915 and 4917. One of them, probably 4915, poses with K3 3394.
Streamlining was for new "Mercury" train, Cleveland - Detroit.

Al Staufer collection

TWENTIETH CENTUR

Other statistics of the train worthy of mention are:

First all-room train in America;
Fastest regular service schedule between New York & Chicago — 16 hours;
Tightlock couplers, Twin Cushion rubber draft gears helped eliminate shocks;
Vestibules that mold into each other and steps that fold up;
Interior colors of rust, blue, tan and grey using natural woods, metals, and leathers;
Every car and every room completely air-conditioned;
Telephone service for communicating with dining car;
Speedometer and odometer in Observation Car;
Decorations include large color maps and scale locomotive models;
Large de luxe "bridal" suite in the observation car with private shower;
Fully equipped service bar as well as barber shop in the lounge car;
Dining car transforms into "night club" after dinner;
Each room in sleeping car has its own toilet;
All beds — six feet five inches long;
All axles, including engine and tender, run on roller bearings;

It was the best of its time, perhaps all time. On June 15th, 1938, the new "Centuries" began their 16 hour service between Chicago and New York.

In 1939 another Hudson received the bullet nose motif. No. 5344 was restreamlined at Collinwood Shop, Cleveland and placed in service between Chicago and Detroit in the "Mercury".

New York Central's "Empire State Express" (Cleveland-New York, Detroit-New York) was one of its top daylight trains. Early in 1941 it was decided to upgrade the train much as the Twentieth Century Limited had been done two years before. Two J3 Hudsons, Nos. 5426 and 5429 were streamlined in a manner to conform with the 32 cars being built by the Edward G. Budd Manufacturing Company. Car interiors were designed by Paul Cret and New York Central engineers. Henry Dreyfuss fashioned the locomotives in a motif similar to the "Century" shrouds, including the 3 foot tender extension.

IMITED

All was ready for the grand inaugural runs. Sunday, December 7, 1941 was the selected day. Press releases were sent but few were ever noticed. The eyes of the world were focused on the Hawaiian Islands. The United States was at war.

The demands of burgeoning war traffic played havoc with the streamliners' shrouds. The name of the game now, was "run trains at peak capacity at all times". Passengers on the "Century" or "Empire" usually had the correct locomotive on the point but equipment was often jumbled with heavy weight cars intermixed with the prevailing streamliners.

Even though Dreyfuss styling made excellent allowances for maintenance, it still wasn't good enough. Permission was soon granted to round house crews for removal of some of the forward cowl and rear skirts to assist in servicing air pump and fire box areas.

Development of the centipede tender late in 1943 dealt the cruellest blow to the aesthetically pure. The superior "PT's" were gradually applied to all streamlined engines. At first they were painted two tone gray, but severe demands ended that luxury. By the final cease fire in August 1945 the

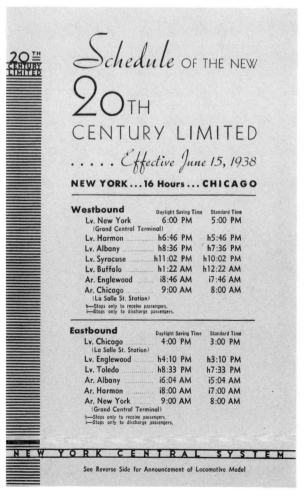

shrouds had deteriorated to a sad state. An unkept steamengine is simply that — unkept. But a dirty cut-up shroud is a disaster to behold.

In late 1945 the superior Niagaras began taking over the elite runs. One "Empire" Hudson, 5426, was assigned to the Chicago-Detroit leg of the Mercury. In this service it was paired for a while with the famous J1e No. 5344.

Almost mercifully, the shrouds were removed, 5445-5454 about 1945-1947, 5426 & 5429 in 1949. In brief summation, this whole streamlining era was much more publicity than substance. Only 15 of New York Central's 4000 locomotives were involved. It was a situation that demanded the right engine to match the new trains not the train to match the engine.

It was brief. It was colorful. It was enjoyable.

5450 new at Schenectady, April, 1938. Devastatingly handsome, but you're fighting a century of history and fact whenever you cover up parts of the engine.

5453 with new PT1 tender (17,500 Gal.-43T) at Beech Grove, August, 1943. Two years later 5453 received PT4 tender (18,000-46T). Beech Grove, Indiana built four PT1 tanks in 1943. Fifty PT4 tenders were built by Lima in 1944-45.

NYC pamphlet extolling the many virtues of their NEW "Century".

J3

5452 at Chicago, September 9, 1940. Just two years old and already the roundhouse crews got their tinsnips out. Actually, removable panels to get at the air pumps.

New York Central

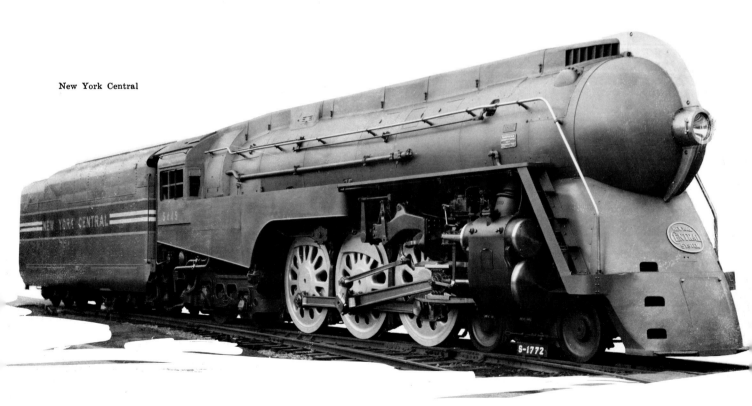

One of the most often asked questions is, what is the exact color of NYC's streamlined Hudsons and passenger cars? Our stock answer is, Lionel's postwar "O" NYC diesels are very close on shades of gray.

New York Central

P. Osbourne in cab of 5449, April, 1938.

June 15, 1938, the first two sections of the new Century leaving Chicago. Above is 5450 with first section.

There was much more hoop-la in Chicago than New York partly because the complete train left right from the heart of the loop while in New York the train wasn't complete till engine change at Harmon.

CHICAGO

Paul Strayer

Above and right, second section departs with 5448. J3 at left may have been for third section, but nobody noticed that. Below, first section arriving in Englewood.

213

Harold Stirton collection

Englewood, 1946. Eastbound Hudson in distance is waiting for W/B 5447 to pull out so it can come in and load, then proceed to New York City. 5447 was built with Boxpok drivers but now has Scullin Disc.

Englewood (Chicago) September 29, 1940. Sound truck is pulled up to serviced Hudsons, we assume to record. Two middle engines are 5318 and 5428.

Don Speidel Jr.

J3 chassis waiting in Collinwood for new boiler shell. All J3's were built with high quality nickel steel riveted boilers, advantages being less weight and less corrosion. Checks and cracks developed in some and those were replaced with high nickel steel all welded boilers. These were put in a big oven (after assembly) to remove stresses.

   Many, possibly all, of the 27 Niagara boilers were replaced because of same problems. We have no exact records on either class, just some J's and possibly all S class.

5454 at Collinwood after being completely repainted.

Jack McGroarty collection

Bob Wayner collection

Special train carrying King George VI and Queen Elizabeth in 1939, along the Hudson River. The consist was a combination of Canadian National and Canadian Pacific cars, plus two private cars of the Governor-General of Canada which their majesties used, with all cars being specially painted for the trip. The King and Queen toured Canada then came down to New York City.

New Century sitting on the wrong track in the electric division. A publicity photo of new equipment.

27 x 41" New York Central travel poster, circa 1927.

New York Central

5451 on display at New York's Worlds Fair, 1939. Note rods painted black.

Al Staufer collection

5451

Edward L. May

April 1, 1945, Elkhart, Ind. War demands played havoc with the sheet metal shrouds.

Chicago, June, 1938. Engine is little over a year old, so must have been present at a grade crossing mishap. All J3's were built with conventional front ends.

Edward L. May

5451 at Harmon, June 18, 1938 for railfan inspection. Left that day at 6:45 P.M. on maiden voyage with No. 25.

Edward L. May

Left and right side views of 5445 taken in 1945 and 46. Near the end of the line for the shrouds. Shabby, but a bit of class under all that grease, tin, and filth.

H. L. Younger

First trip through Erie, Pa. for new Empire State Express. Right: 5429 after streamlining.

The boys look 'er over at Erie, Pa.

H. L. Younger

Signs at left and right say "Danger Keep Out When Coupling". Sign in middle says "Danger, Keep-Off, steam and hot water, booster exhaust."

They keep a Super Service Station for New York Central Locomotives

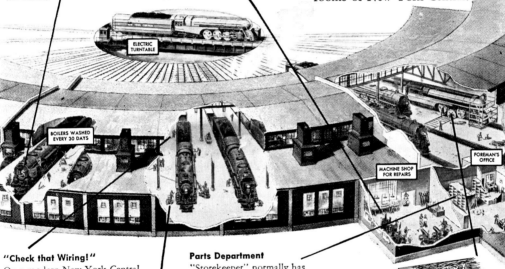

THE run ends. Engineer and fireman climb down from the cab, and a "hostler" takes over. Under his expert hand, 350 tons of pulsing steel move obediently off to the roundhouse...that super service station for locomotives.

Here, mechanics, electricians, pipe-fitters, specialists in many crafts work day and night...inspecting, repairing, lubricating and adjusting the engines of New York Central's motive power fleet.

Today, with modern machines and electrical aids, they're cutting hours from maintenance time...keeping engines longer on the job to move war traffic. And tomorrow these roundhouse teams will apply their war-born efficiency to servicing still finer locomotives now taking shape in the designing rooms of New York Central.

Looking "Under the Hood"
Inspector opens locomotive front, and steps inside to examine smokebox. Rigid check-up keeps New York Central engines working efficiently despite heavy war loads.

Electric "Detective"
Before invisible cracks in steel can grow and cause a breakdown, Machinists locate them with an electric detector called the Magnaflux. "An ounce of prevention is worth tons of cure" on New York Central.

"Check that Wiring!"
On a modern New York Central steam locomotive, Electricians have many things to check... from the headlight to the electric Train Stop, the wonderful guardian that would halt train *automatically* if danger signal were passed.

Parts Department
"Storekeeper" normally has thousands of parts on hand. They range from driving wheels to tiny springs for Valve-Speed Indicator...a device that keeps a safety and efficiency log for each locomotive.

Lubrication Job — Locomotive Size!
Roundhouse Grease Cup Fillers use lubricating guns so large they are moved about on wheels. Grease and oil are forced out by high pressure air from nearby power house.

"Change those Tires!"
Locomotives have steel tires. When tires need changing, electric Drop Table lowers 32 tons of driving wheels and whisks them to service track...50% faster than old methods of wheel removal.

FREE! NEW, ENLARGED BOOKLET. "Behind the Scenes of a Railroad at War" with 13 fascinating cutaway pictures. Write Room 1223E, 466 Lexington Ave., New York 17, N.Y.

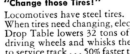

BUY MORE WAR BONDS
NEW YORK CENTRAL
THE WATER LEVEL ROUTE

New York Central ad, June, 1945.

Central New York Chapter NRHS

Above: 5426 west of Syracuse on trial or exhibition trip in late Nov., 1941. Engine, tender and 9 cars all matching and perfect.
Below: 5426 again with 16 car train taking water at Scotia (west of Schenectady) about 1946. Most obvious changes are: PT tender, removal of firebox skirt and other cars mixed in with the Budd coaches.

Ed Nowak - New York Central

Publicity photo of new train with cylinder cocks open for dramatic effect. Passing Breakneck Mt.

New York Central

5429 at Montrose, N.Y. April 7, 1946. This is not the "Empire". 51 & 50 are being handled by the massive 4-8-4 Niagaras now.

Edward L. May

5426, Chicago, August 10, 1947. 5426 now doing Detroit-Chicago "Mercury" service with J1e 5344. First and second drivers disc and rear is Web-Spoke. Cars appear to be pretty good mixture of rebuilt Mercury and conventional streamlined coaches.

Lee A. Hastman collection

Westfield, N.Y., 1942. Eastbound Empire State Hudson 5426 meets Westfield & North Western interurban. Lots of nostalgia but that's about all we know. Why the old combine-coach cut in behind this hot-shot Express engine? If we could see rest of train, then reasonable guess would be possible.

William F. Herrmann collection

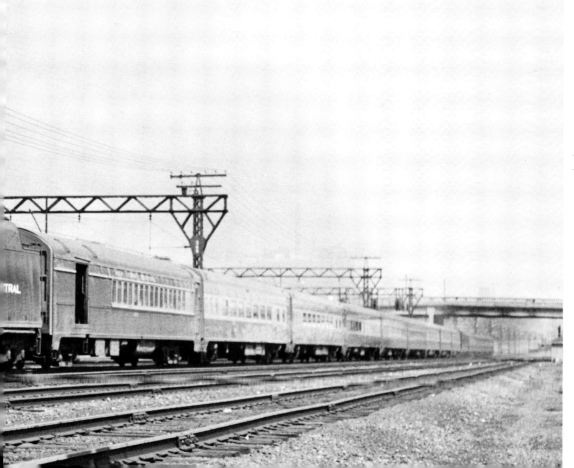

THE

MERCURY

EMPIRE STATE EXPRESS

Bert Pennypacker

Winter of '42. Sunrise glory with 5426 on Empire just before entering Oscawana tunnel. Train has all original equipment and is still new.

EMPIRE STATE EXPRESS

Dick Jacobs

This is the way we saw them, mass of steam, steel and smoke plunging toward us at 80 mph. Three or four CHUGS that lift you off your feet then wham! Blast out the other side and disappear in a distant haze of smoke and dust.
Westbound at Syracuse, N.Y., 1946.

Harmon, N.Y., June 16, 1946. Still pretty much of the original tin left. It's almost as if the engine underneath were trying to shed this unreal mask. Nice when new but just plain didn't work out too well. Note turbogenerator by trailing truck.

Edward L. May

5429 in Chicago, where the Empire State Express did not go.

William A. Raia collection

Edward L. May

Rensselaer, N.Y. 5426 waits for Albany Harmon job. No more Empire State's for this loco as the new massive Niagaras were in service. May 4, 1946.

5426 after streamlining shroud was removed. Immediately thereafter, Worthington feedwater heater applied and reverse gear moved outside the frame. Engine looks relaxed compared with the photo above.

Bob Yanosey collection

THE MOST FAM

)US

New York Central

Obviously, within the most famous class of locomotives in the world, there had to be some which, for a variety of reasons, were to stand above the rest. 5315 was immortalized by the disastrous wreck at Little Falls, New York. 5405, the first of the "Super Hudsons", received the usual publicity accorded those who come first. The streamlined clan were ballyhooed to drum up interest for the modern trains they would haul. One would assume, and quite logically, that laurels should go to much tested and publicized Hudson number one — 5200.

Not so, for it befell the last J1 built, No. 5344, to achieve the undisputed claim as The Most Famous of the most famous. We can explain the reason for her fame and why it was this particular locomotive. Actually it could have been either 5343 or 5344 since they were the only J1's built with all roller bearings engine and tender (except trailing trucks).

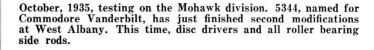

October, 1935, testing on the Mohawk division. 5344, named for Commodore Vanderbilt, has just finished second modifications at West Albany. This time, disc drivers and all roller bearing side rods.

5344

J1e 5344 became the most famous of the famous because it was the last J1e built and because all the latest improvements were built in, particularly Timken roller bearings. They graced all engine and tender axles except pony wheels, which were SKF, and trailing truck which were conventional solids. Side rods and valve gear parts were also brass solid bearings.

Sister engine 5343 was next to last J1e built and also equipped with roller bearings. SKF on all engine and tender axles except trailing truck, which were solids.

AMERICAN LOCOMOTIVE COMPANY
NEW YORK

Class, 464 S 350 (Hudson Type
Road Number, 5344

BUILT FOR THE NEW YORK CENTRAL.

GAUGE OF TRACK	CYLINDERS		DRIVING WHEEL DIAMETER	BOILER		FIRE BOX		TUBES		
	Diam.	Stroke		Inside Dia.	Pressure	Length	Width	Number	Diameter	Length
4'-8½"	25"	28"	79"	82 7/16"	225 lbs.	130"	90 ¼"	37 / 201	2¼" / 3½"	20'-6"

WHEEL BASE			WEIGHT IN WORKING ORDER—POUNDS					
Driving	Engine	Engine & Tender	Leading	Driving	Trailing		Engine	Tender
					FRONT	REAR		
14'-0"	40'-4"	83'-7½"	63500	189000	44000	53500	350000	300300

FUEL	EVAPORATING SURFACES, SQ. FT.					SUPERHEATING SURFACE SQUARE FT.	GRATE AREA SQ. FT.	MAXIMUM TRACTIVE POWER		FACTOR OF ADHESION	
Kind	Tubes	Flues	Fire Box	Arch Tubes	Total			Engine	Booster	Drivers	Trailer
Soft Coal	800	3403	244	37	4484	1951	81.5	42300 lbs	10900 lbs	4.47	4.91

Tender Type, 12-Wheeled   Capacity, Water, 14000 Gals.   Fuel, 28 Tons

ORDER No. S-1716
November, 1931

THE COMMODORE VANDERBILT

On a bitter cold day in December, 1934, the first streamlined steam engine in the United States poses for the official series of company photographs at Harmon Yards.

In the summer of 1934, 5344 was pulled from service, sent to West Albany, and fitted with the first sheet metal shroud in America.

Design was developed by the "Case School of Applied Science" (Cleveland), and, true to archaic traditions, they completely covered her up — tender and all. "Commodore Vanderbilt" (her name) was painted gun metal gray with aluminum trim and letters; a motif that proved to be the color style setter for following streamlined New York Central engines and trains. Lacey spoked drivers were the only aesthetic violation on an otherwise not too bad a-lookin' machine.

This shroud was no haphazard, slap-on affair. On the contrary, it was well planned and functional. Several hinged panels made maintenance points quite accessible and a grilled recess on top of the cowling aided the updraft of smoke. Two areas where streamlining definitely aided the operation of a steam locomotive were air flow and insulation. We know of no tests to prove the effect of wind resistance, but claims of 2%+ aid under certain conditions certainly do not seem excessive. And there is no denying that an outer shell certainly helped minimize heat loss. But, the disadvantages of weight, cost and upkeep far outweighed these benefits. But publicity was the game, not practicality.

Getting back to 5344: first assignment was "The Century" (what else), on the 233 mile Chicago-Toledo run; inaugural trip was February 19, 1935. After working Nos. 25 and 26 for about 8 months, she was sent to West Albany Shops for further improvements. Boiler pressure was increased to 250 lbs., roller bearings were applied to side rods and disc drivers replaced the spoked originals. New York

Central was constantly pressed to up-grade performance; and, clearly, 5344 was the engine most often tinkered with. In this garb, our star performed until July, 1939.

It would be well to mention here that 5344 was a West End (west of Buffalo) engine; which accounts, in part, why we have so few pictures of her in service. Had she worked out of Harmon, you can bet your socks that the New York City boys would have remedied that deficiency.

In 1938, ten new streamlined Hudsons took over the glamour runs; so, back to Collinwood (July 1939) went "Commodore Vanderbilt". This time she emerged with a shroud similar to the Henry Dreyfuss styled 5445-5454. Newly dressed 5344 bumped a streamlined Pacific from the Chicago-Detroit leg of the "Mercury".

Her streamlined days ended abruptly when a sand truck raced her to a grade crossing in East Chicago, Oct. 1945. It was a tie ! She then received the huge PT tender that was being fitted to many of the Hudson Fleet. And this is the way she finished her days, certainly bearing little resemblance to the elegant machine that rolled out of Schenectady just twenty-three years before.

One would assume that all these aforegoing events would assuredly be sufficient to catapult 5344 to the top. But there is more, much more. In a word, TOYS. Yes it was toys, children's toys that did more to immortalize No. 5344 than all the streamliners in America. So much so, that we have devoted a separate chapter in this book to just that subject.

5344 is gone — all the Hudsons are gone. Maybe, just maybe, their fame will better reach full measure through story and picture. We are more fragile than they, and who can tell — maybe someday — — just maybe.

New York Central

The first all-roller bearing steam locomotive in America was Timken's "Four Aces" built by Alco in April, 1930. Central followed with two J1e's in late 1931.

5344 "Commodore" on display in Boston's South Station.

Norton D. Clark

New York Central

"Commodore Vanderbilt" and DeWitt Clinton replica, publicity shot at West Albany, December, 1934. Must say it looks mighty good for 40 years ago.

On display in Manhattan's Grand Central Terminal. This is the first application we've seen of NYC Lines oval on a locomotive.

Central New York Chapter NRHS

5344 passing by the old station at Syracuse heading west, Jan. 10, 1935. Great Steel Fleet passes here in the dark, so train just could be Empire State Express — or display run.

5344

Rare, rare, rare shot of "Commodore" moving, possibly out of East St. Louis, Illinois. If so, it's an exhibition train as this engine did not serve on the Big Four at this time.

Lee A. Hastman collection

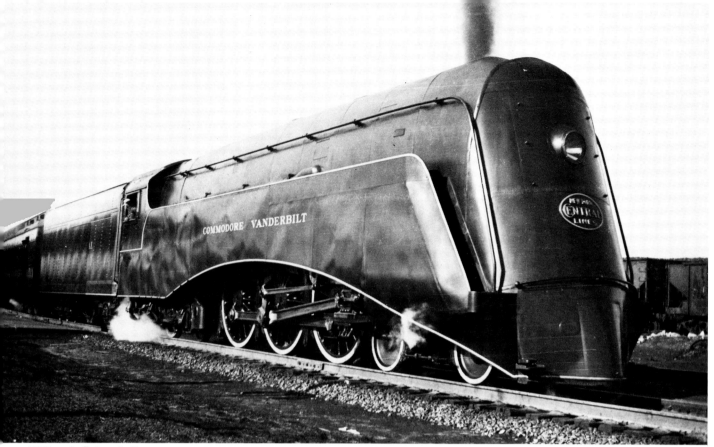

William A. Raia collection

In revenue service in original livery on Twentieth Century at Englewood, Ill. This shroud held up much better than the later ones, because it was one of a kind..

Scratch board rendering of new streamlined train. In this technique the artist works with india ink on a special board surfaced with hard chalk. He has the option of working on it in the conventional drawing method or painting areas black and scratching out the white areas. This commercial artist did both.

While on the subject, no artist can totally divorce himself from the style and mood of the times — and the times themselves. This sketch is obviously mid-1930's. We like it.

New York Central

COMMODORE VANDERBILT

New York Central

Commodore Vanderbilt (5344) made its inaugural run with "Century" on February 19, 1935. After about 8 months loco was sent back to West Albany for disc drivers, roller bearing side rods and steam pressure raised to 250 lbs. She sits here at West Albany with the alterations just completed.

Edward L. May

Cover on coal pile accordioned back to allow complete filling of the bunker. No question about it, this was New York Central's experimental Hudson — all the way.

New York Central

Central's publicity brochure stated, "It is believed the streamlining of this Hudson whenever the engine is operated at speeds of 70 to 90 mph or more, will effect a decrease in head air resistance of 35 to 36 percent, which is expected to be reflected in a saving of fuel."

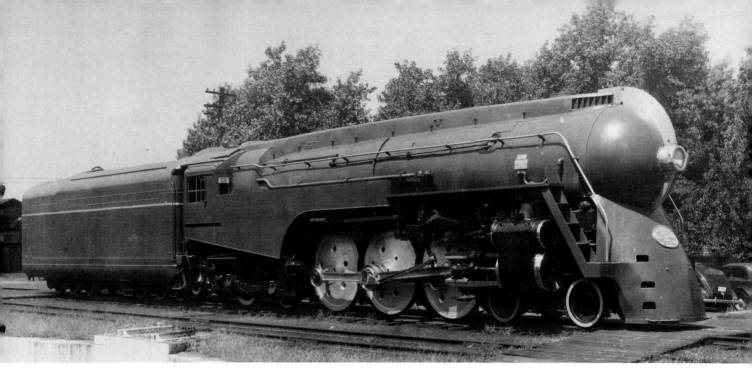

J1e 5344 had so many improvements that except for combustion chamber, she might as well have been a J3 super Hudson. In 1939, at Collinwood, she traded in her Commodore shroud for the "20thCentury" style shroud, only difference being that she had raised running board and no cover over the pumps.

Don Speidel Jr.

THE MERCURY

Edward L. May

In this garb she handled the Chicago-Detroit leg of the "Mercury". Shown here at Chicago's Illinois Central Station.

William A. Raia collection

At this time Michigan Central trains used the Illinois Central station in Chicago, instead of LaSalle Street. New Mercury engine is on display. Engine at left is I.C.'s 1157 Pacific.

Our star blasting out of Detroit's Central Station for Chicago. The Cleveland run was powered by a streamlined Pacific, so we must assume Chicago runs were heavier.

243

Lee A. Hastman collection

5344 in Mercury streamlining.

In our vast assemblage of Hudson photographs this is the only one we have of a Hudson undergoing major backshop rebuilding. And lucky for us it is 5344. Various brackets that hold up the original Commodore shroud can be seen. Note the smoke box depression for Coffin feedwater heater. Also good view of air pump bracket castings.

This is another of these "wish we could walk into the picture and browse around". All parts are chalk marked so they get back to original engine.

Jack McGroarty collection

R. Ganger

Ashes to Ashes,
dust to dust,
steel to steel,
return it must.

Above is 5344 at Englewood, Ill., October 1, 1946, back in familiar form. We won't even count the changes but at this stage 5344, the last J1e built is more a super J3.
Through her entire life she was always more "something in between", always tinkered with, always streamlined, and always a HUDSON.

No. 5344

HUDSON WRE

CKS

There are many among the rail enthusiast fraternity who consider any discussion of disaster a breach of faith or something sacrilegious. We do not delve in the macabre sense, we merely discuss it as part of the total Hudson story.

Our records are very scant, we only know of two major accidents but the Hudson record must be little short of spectacular. Here's why—Visualize a fleet of 275 locomotives, each rolling up between 10,000 and 20,000 high speed miles a month for 25 years. IN OVER ONE BILLION MILES ONLY ONE NYC HUDSON WAS PERMANENTLY DESTROYED BECAUSE OF ACCIDENT. Truly phenomenal!

We will only analyze the spectacular disaster that took a fearful toll in human life and, incidentally, destroyed the only Hudson.

Lake Shore wreck near Huron, Ohio about 1945 or 1946. 5304, speeding along with mail and express, hit a motorized hand car causing engine to tip over and send cars sprawling every which way.

Our account of this wreck is not authenticated but those who remember it tell us the engineer was killed.

247

H. L. Younger

THE WRECK AT LITTLE FALLS

April 19, 1940 about 11:30 p.m. The westbound New York—Chicago. "Lake Shore Limited", train No. 19, was about 72 miles west of Albany running about 20 minutes late approaching Little Falls, N.Y. at a speed of 74 m.p.h. Locomotive was Hudson 5315, the first Jle built. In the cab are engineer Jesse Earl, Fireman J. Y. Smith and Road Foreman of Engines, Bayreuther. The train of 15 cars consisted of one express car, one baggage car, two coaches, four Pullman sleeping cars, one dining car, five Pullman sleeping cars, and one coach (in that order).

Ahead lies rather sharp Gulf Curve, due to bend in Mohawk River, about 1000 feet through, 8" track superelevation and strict speed limit of 45 m.p.h. Train No. 19 slowed from 74 m.p.h. to 59 m.p.h. at the beginning of the curve. As it entered the curve there was a thrust from the train throwing 5315 into the air slamming it against a stone retaining wall. The second and fifth car proceeded by the engine and remained upright on the track. The four next-to-last cars derailed but remained upright and the last four cars did not derail. Cars one, three, four, six and seven slammed into the engine and tender.

31 people were killed including the engineer and fireman, and 51 were injured. Miraculously, Road Foreman of Engines Bayreuther lived through the carnage.

What happened? 59 m.p.h. is certainly not the critical speed on a 45 m.p.h. curve. Actually tipover speed was estimated at 78 m.p.h. and could well have exceeded that. Everything was in perfect order; track, signals, and all equipment. Engineer and fireman were veterans with excellent records: further, they ran that curve hundreds of times.

The ICC investigation of June 1940 summed it up with this terse conclusion: "This accident was caused by excessive speed on a sharp curve combined with a run-in of slack resulting from the throttle being closed suddenly."

Usual practice was to make brake pipe reduction (train air brakes) about 3000 ft. before reaching curve until speed was about 40 m.p.h. then proceed through curve at not over 45 m.p.h. No brakes were to be applied in the curve.

Survivor Bayreuther relates what happened: "Engineer Earl made brake pipe reduction before entering curve but only enough to reduce speed to

248

New York Central

5315

Above: Wreck at Little Falls the following morning with upright cars pulled away to the right.
Left: Work trains clearing the wreckage. Note, the broken stack among other things on 5315.
Below: 5315 on the "Iroquois". Shortest lived Hudson of them all — wrecked at Little Falls almost 9 years to the day after building.

Rail Photo Service

Right: coach, and below, Pullman after being pulled from the wreckage at Little Falls.

about 60 m.p.h. After crossing to the right side of the cab, he (Bayreuther) instructed the engineman to reduce pressure further, but Earl suddenly closed the throttle instead."

The engine was already in the curve about 15 m.p.h. over the speed limit so when the throttle was shut the surge or heavy run-in from the 15 cars literally buckled the engine and tender into the air.

It was reasoned that if he had not closed the throttle, the train would have proceeded through the curve O.K. So in effect, the engineer happened to do the one thing that could have caused a wreck at that instant.

Why?- Was he nervous with the Road Foreman aboard? Was he distracted before entering the curve? Did he react unnaturally when he sensed the danger and heard the order? We'll never know.

As they say in the automotive world, "5315 was totalled". Rock penetrated the firebox wrapper sheet and the resulting explosion destroyed the entire firebox and grate area. The cast steel frame was bent and broken in two places. No. 3 driver was torn loose. Everything was destroyed and 5315 was scrapped—the only Hudson to be lost in service.

CANASTOTA, N.Y.

Next to Little Falls, the most spectacular accident directly involving a Hudson was the explosion of 5450 on No. 26 "Twentieth Century Limited" eastbound between 4 and 5 a.m., September 7, 1943 on the Mohawk Div. at Canastota, N.Y.

The streamlined Hudson ruptured so violently that most of the boiler and cab were separated from the running gear. About all that remained on the chassis was the boiler front, throttle, superheater header and superheater tubes.

We don't have the official report but wrecks of this type were almost always caused by low water. Boilers were usually built to a safety factor of four or five i.e. able to withstand 4 or 5 times their working pressure, so structural failure is nearly impossible. No boiler, however, is built to withstand the force of a crown sheet (top of firebox) overheated by low water.

The temptation is great for crews to run with low water since any steam locomotive is nearly twice the machine with thin water covering the crown sheet than too full a boiler. When the crown sheet

Air view of Little Falls clean-up operations and resultant traffic jam. The morning after the accident the crowd on the scene was estimated at over 100,000.

C. A. Peterson

Would you believe this?   C. A. Peterson

Water boils at 212°F. at sea level atmospheric pressure. It boils at a much higher temperature under pressure. Release that pressure and all the water turns to instant steam.

ruptures the release or lowering of pressure causes all the boiler water to turn into instant steam. This enormous release of energy takes the path of least resistance which is usually downward through the firebox grate area. Such was probably the case with 5450.

The engineer, George Pierce and fireman, Jack Larsen of Syracuse and traveling fireman Charles Ricker of Albany were all killed.

There were 17 cars in the train; all derailed except the last 3. The head car was an RPO mail car with 11 clerks working, and only two of them were slightly injured. There were no injuries throughout the rest of the train, in fact, several of the passengers in the last three cars slept through it all and did not even wake up until a couple of hours later.

Even though the boiler and cab were destroyed, 5450 was rebuilt, and reboilered in Sept. 1944. We don't know if 5450 was streamlined or not but if she wasn't, then that would have been the first to lose its shroud.

GRADE CROSSINGS

New York Central's ratio of grade crossing accidents must have been quite substantial because of the many high speed train miles over multiple tracked mainline that crossed thousands of heavily travelled roadways.

No honor, but it's doubtful if they were second to any other railroad, even the Pennsylvania.

Fallen monarch. 5304 on its side at Huron, Ohio.

253

Hudson 5422 after the wreck of #21 at Oneida, N.Y., October, 1950. We have no details of this accident but we observe the fireman's side of the cab ripped out.

Ed Nowak - New York Central

Paul Slawson

254

ROCHESTER

Paul Slawson

This picture and opposite page bottom are of 5414 (?) on #8 "Wolverine" after plunging off embankment 1000 feet west of Rochester, New York station. Accident was on 45 mph curve. Engineer was killed and fireman crippled.

Heck of a way to find out, but it does give us a view of a J3 Hudson turned upside down, revealing brake rigging and other innards we never see. Note PT tender pilot truck below pony truck of engine.

THE GREAT STEEL

FLEET

Al Staufer

During the earlier days of this century and particularly in the span of years between the two World Wars railroad passenger train operation in this country soared to heights never before known and never to be known again. During these brief years when limited trains and flyers raced across the broad land there was no one with a bigger or finer fleet of luxury name trains than the New York Central. Beginning with the inauguration of the "Empire State Express" in 1891, the creation of the railroad's imaginative General Passenger Agent and public relations expert George H. Daniels, and continuing with his inspired "20th Century Limited", the Cen tral had the traffic potential and the plant to operate these trains and did it "to the hilt". These limiteds of the NYC Lines were to its four-track main line what the "Berengaria", Aquitania", "France" and later "Normandie" and "Queen Mary" were to the North Atlantic shipping lanes. Both these modes of transportation have become victims of the air age but they were, in their day, each the ultimate in travel.

Listed below are the names and numbers of some of these trains of reknown along with some notes on their equipment as culled from old time-

New York Central passenger car storage yard behind Cleveland Union Terminal. Note the open platform, two tone gray heavyweight business car.

tables and cobwebbed memories. Many carried observation lounge cars sporting tail signs and practically all featured diners or diner-lounge cars for at least the meal hour portions of their runs. It was the practice in the '20's to cut diners in and out of trains enroute for meal times and even the "Century" westbound had its diner cut out at Syracuse and another cut back in at Toledo for breakfast. The same practice eastbound saw the diner cut out at Ashtabula and another put on at Syracuse. With the depression and an effort to effect economies by eliminating as much switching as possible the diners began to operate through from one terminal to another unless only one meal was required. This same economy saw the disappearance except on a small number of limiteds of the observation car and its name-bearing drumhead. One plus as a result of this cutback in excessive terminal switching was a cut in running time for many trains. Most of the limited trains in the '20's boasted "Pullman Cars Only-No Coach Passengers Carried" not to mention the other familiar timetable note "An Extra Fare is Charged on This Train". As with the observation cars, the depression also sounded the knell for the extra fare except on the "Century" and in an effort to increase traffic during those lean years of the early '30's coaches were added to almost all trains, though the advent of the reclining seat de luxe coach was still a few years distant. Where the list shows "Pullman Cars Only" this applies mostly to the '20's era.

Not all of these trains operated throughout the Hudson Age and the same names were applied to different services at different times. It is hoped this list might conjure up fond memories of a once enjoyed speedy run behind a 'J' or perhaps of a fine meal in one of the diners enroute or, perhaps, a pleasant interlude on the back observation platform watching the countryside recede in a maze of dust and cinders at 80 m.p.h.

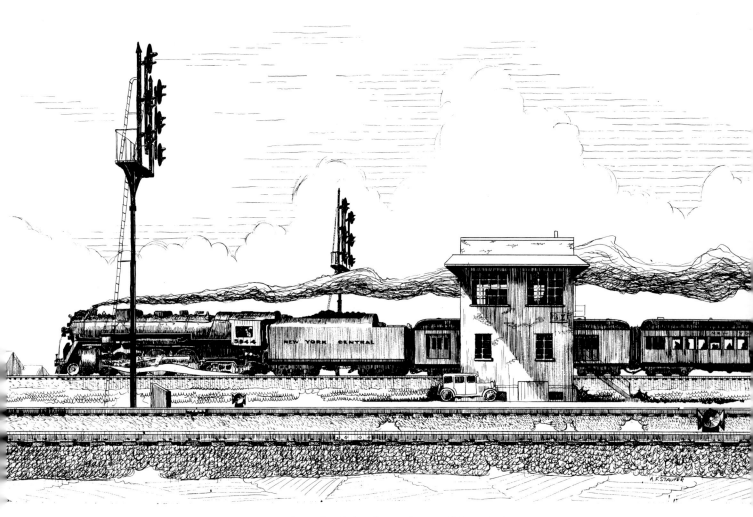

Pen sketch by the author — "No. 6 by".

THE GREAT STEEL FLEET

Train Numbers	Name	Remarks
1 & 2	Day Coach De Luxe	Inaugurated 1928 as an all-coach daylight train between New York and Buffalo in both directions making many stops omitted by the "Empire". Later carried parlor cars and also on occasion cars to Cleveland and sleepers for Chicago via a connection with #3, "Chicago Express".
1 & 2	The Cayuga	Successor to Day Coach De Luxe, cut back to Syracuse and still later to Utica.
3	Chicago Express	Early morning 24-hour train New York to Chicago plug with sleepers and coaches plus a New York-Cleveland parlor car. Picked up Chicago and Cincinnati sleepers at Buffalo and other Chicago sleepers at Cleveland.
3 & 2 (Later 1 & 2)	Pacemaker	Central's reply to Pennsy's "Trailblazer". Inaugurated during World's Fair year of 1939. Featured rebuilt equipment until 1948. All-coach New York-Chicago with a.m. arrivals.
3 & 4	James Whitcomb Riley	Inaugurated 1941 in both directions between Cincinnati and Chicago requiring only one set of equipment. Departed Cincinnati early a.m. and returned leaving the Windy City late afternoon. Assigned first Budd-built coaches on railroad.
4	New York Limited	Pullman Cars Only Cleveland to New York with early a.m. arrival in New York. Later as "New York Special" carried Chicago sleepers for New York as well as some for Boston.
X4	Fast Mail	Pullman Cars Only. One of five 20-hour trains with extra early a.m. arrival in New York from Chicago. Extra fare train that only ran for a short time.
5	Mohawk	Pre-noon New York City departure with sleepers and coaches for Chicago adding along the route sleepers from Auburn, Buffalo, Pittsburgh and Cleveland for Chicago. Parlor car on New York-Buffalo portion of run. Featured $7.20 extra fare for the 22-hour New York-Chicago trip.
6	Fifth Avenue Special	For years a favorite for early arrivals in New York from Chicago. Pullman Cars Only on this limited.
7	Westerner	During the '20's this was one of the few coach trains available for New York-Chicago patrons and no extra fare, either BUT featuring a 28-hour trip in straight-back coaches. Carried an assortment of sleepers and parlors along the route.
7 & 16	Motor City Special	Later #315 and #316. This was the Michigan Central's overnighter between Detroit & Chicago. During World War II sleeper restrictions operated daylight runs.
8	Wolverine	Longtime Chicago to New York favorite via M.C.R.R. One of the 1929 speed-ups to 20-hours. All Pullman with cars also from Detroit to Boston.
9	Fast Mail	New York to Chicago mailtrain. No through coaches. Various times carried Cleveland and Toledo sleepers for Chicago.
10	Mohawk	Later afternoon Chicago departure with coaches and sleepers for mid-afternoon in New York. Carried Chicago sleepers to Buffalo and Rochester for morning arrivals.
10	Water Level Limited	Latter day Chicago to New York coaches and sleepers with late morning arrival N.Y.
11 & 12	Southwestern Limited	Pullmans Only on this New York-St. Louis limited in both directions. Dates back to the '90's as one of the road's "crack" trains. Cars from Boston and New York for Indianapolis, Cleveland, Cincinnati as well as St. Louis.
13	New England Wolverine	Later #33. Pullmans Only from Boston to Detroit and Chicago via M.C.R.R.
15 & 16	Ohio State Limited	Longtime New York and Boston to Cincinnati limited with eastbound counterpart known as "Hudson River Limited" (2nd #26) until late '20's.
16	Prairie State	Sleepers Chicago to New York and coaches Chicago to New York on #142 east of Buffalo. Also, sleepers Cleveland to Albany, Rochester, Buffalo, Toronto. Mid-afternoon departure from Chicago and mid-afternoon arrival in New York.
17	Wolverine	Longrunning New York-Chicago flyer via Michigan Central. One of four westbound 20-hour extra fare trains in 1929 speed-up.
18	Knickerbocker Special	Big Four train with sleepers but no through coaches St. Louis and Cincinnati to New York, Boston, Albany, Buffalo with parlor cars on daylight portions of run. Early p.m. from St. Louis and late afternoon into New York.

19 & 20	Lake Shore Limited	THE Luxury New York-Chicago Limited prior to the "Century". Pullman Cars Only with late p.m. departure from New York and Chicago. Oddly, not included in 1929 speed-up when four westbounds and five eastbounds were carded for 20-hours.
20	The Cayuga	One of many trains to bear this name. Earlier called "The New Yorker". Early a.m. departure from Cleveland to New York with parlors arriving late evening. Victim of depression.
21	Cleveland Limited	Exactly as its name implies. Overnight Pullman Cars Only New York and Boston to Cleveland. Later #57.
21	North Star	Overnight train carrying sleepers for Cleveland, Toronto and North Country points from New York. Successor to #27, "Toronto Limited".
23	Western Express	New York-Chicago train featuring dinner time departure with coaches and sleepers making all the stops. One of the few trains with through coaches during the '20's Pullman Cars Only era.
23	Knickerbocker	Short-lived mid-'30's 23-hour New York-St. Louis train with dinner hour departure from New York. Carried also a Cincinnati sleeper for connection at Galion.
24	Knickerbocker	Big Four train from St. Louis later extended from Cleveland through to New York carrying cars east of Cleveland originally handled on train #68, "Commodore".
25 & 26	20th Century Limited	The Railroad advertised this superbly named train as its "Luxury Liner On Wheels", "World's Premier Train", "World's Most Distinguished Train". It was all of that and more; it was "extra fare", "extra fast", "extra fine" and the world's most reknowned limited. Operated from June 15, 1902 until discontinued December 2, 1967, a victim not of the private motor car or bus competition but of the jet plane. At various times a 20-hour and for some years a speedy 16-hour train between New York and Chicago it was all-Pullman until its last decade when it fell to carrying sleeper coaches and coaches. Carried cars west from Albany from the Boston section until it became an all-room streamline and in June 1938 after which Boston cars were handled separately in the "New England States". Featured all the extras that went with the extra fare - "maid service", "secretary", "barber shop", "valet", etc.
27	Toronto Limited	Overnight Pullmans for Toronto, Cleveland, Adirondacks from New York and Boston later handled in train #21, "North Star".
27 & 28	New England States	Boston-Chicago flyer inaugurated 1938 when Boston section of "Century" was discontinued. Pullman Cars Only when "Paul Revere" was operating.
29	Niagara	Inaugurated 1926 with a late evening departure from New York with sleepers for Buffalo, Niagara Falls and Chicago via M.C.R.R. Featured a 24-hour Niagara Falls layover sleeper for a time.
30	Niagara	Eastbound counterpart of the "Toronto Limited" with overnight Pullmans to New York from Toronto and upstate New York points with Boston connection, later "Iroquois". In later years had St. Lawrence Division sleepers.
30 & 31	Twilight Limited	Earlier #25 and #26 this was the Michigan Central's Chicago-Detroit all-parlor car equivalent of the Central's "Empire". The depression saw coaches added to this train.
33	Buffalonian	Longtime overnight New York to Buffalo train. Discontinued c1930.
33 & 34	The Michigan	Morning departures between Detroit and Chicago. Discontinued after "Mercury" placed in service.
34	Buffalo-New York Express	Overnight sleepers and coaches Buffalo to New York with North Country through sleepers to New York. Makeups for summer Sunday nights showed 34 assigned sleepers for New York, 14 alone from Lake Placid.
34	Seneca	Successor to Day Coach De Luxe eastbound, Buffalo to New York.
34	*Cayuga	Postwar Buffalo-New York with Buffalo, Syracuse and Utica sleepers.
35	Detroit Mail	Buffalo, Detroit and St. Lawrence Division sleepers from New York but no through coaches.
35	20-Hour Chicagoan	Short-lived late evening 20-hour train New York to Chicago. Succeeded by Train #59, "Iroquois".
35	Iroquois	Late evening coaches and sleepers via connection for St. Louis, Cleveland and Detroit from New York and Boston. Carried St. Lawrence Division sleepers and coach (See Train #59).

#	Name	Description
36	Seneca	Early a.m. New York City arrival with sleepers and coaches from Rochester, Oswego and Syracuse.
36	Genesee	Carried Syracuse and Utica sleepers and coaches to New York plus sleepers from Auburn Road, Adirondack Division and D&H.
37 & 38	Advance 20th Century	Short lived (2-1/2 years) and almost forgotten 20-hour New York-Chicago relief train for the "Century". Operated about 45 minutes in advance and boasted all the same luxuries.
38	Missourian	Sleepers and coaches St. Louis to the east, New York and Boston. Daylight trip across New York state with late afternoon arrival in New York. Sleepers cut in and out along the route. Became known among rail fans as the "late train" instead of "Missourian" due to poor on-time performance.
39 & 40	North Shore Limited	Longtime New York-Chicago express via Michigan Central. Known as "Exposition Flyer" during 1933 season of Chicago World's Fair. One of the "Pullman Cars Only" variety before the depression era.
41	Cayuga (later (Knickerbocker)	Placed in service 1905 as a New York-Buffalo train with a post-noon departure. It was known for a time as "Second Empire Limited", "Number Forty One", and later as "Cayuga and finally "Knickerbocker". Carried cars for Chicago and St. Louis.
42	Boston Express	Overnight Buffalo to Boston with Buffalo and Syracuse cars and even a Buffalo to Springfield sleeper.
43	South Shore Express	On B&A known as "New York State Express", it was counterpart of #42 aforementioned. On Albany-Buffalo portion for a while known as "Fast Mail". Later "South Shore Express" to Chicago with assortment of equipment.
44	New York City Special	Later "Niagara". Michigan Central sleepers from Detroit, Bay City, Grand Rapids to New York with an early a.m. arrival.
46	Boston Express	Pullman Cars Only during the glory days and sometimes known as "Berkshire" and lastly "Interstate Express". Cars from Chicago, Detroit and Buffalo for Boston mid-morning arrival.
47 & 48	Detroiter	As its name implies, THE overnighter, Pullmans Only.
49	Berkshire	Sleepers only for Chicago, Detroit and Buffalo from Boston when the J-2's were new.
49	Advance Knickerbocker	Latter day early afternoon departure from New York with sleepers for St. Louis and Cincinnati and same from Boston succeeding "Berkshire" on that part of run.
50 & 51	Empire State Express	Daniel's first brain-child in 1890 became known round the world when Charlie Hogan with the 999 hit 112-1/2 miles per hour in 1893. Carried parlor cars, coaches and diner between New York and Buffalo and sometimes as far as Cleveland and for some years before its streamlining in 1941 also carried equipment for North Country territory. At various times had equipment for Toronto and Detroit. The parlor observation went to Toronto for several years. Streamlined in 1941 (inaugurated Pearl Harbor Day), this Budd-built train ran its capacity 17 cars for a full decade before gradually falling casualty to the New York State Thruway, among other things.
54	Buffalonian	Jack-of-all-trades Buffalo to New York overnighter with sleepers and coaches, picking up cars from other trains and Adirondack Div. sleepers.
54	Mohawk	Early morning local-express Buffalo to New York carrying sleepers from other trains and D&H parlor cars from the North.
55	Advance Empire State Express	Placed in service when Empire State was streamlined to handle more local New York State traffic and Adirondack and St. Lawrence Division cars formerly on #51.
56	DeWitt Clinton	Longtime from Chicago (via M.C.R.R.) and Toledo on main line featuring latest arrival of any through train into Grand Central, around midnight. For some time handled probably longest parlor car run on road (possibly in country), Car #475 from Toledo to New York.
58	Seneca	Earlier the "Metropolitan", a train Buffalo to New York, early evening arrival with connecting sleepers picked up at Buffalo. Later "Niagara" on New York Central and "Canad an" on Michigan Central connection.
57 & 58	Cleveland Limited	Westbound formerly was #21 and the eastbound was created to relieve several other trains of their Cleveland-New York sleepers. No coach passengers carried. Pullmans Only.
59	Iroquois	Pullmans Only. Very late departure with sleepers New York to Detroit, Chicago, Buffalo. Later "Chicagoan".

61	Seneca	Almost midnight New York-Syracues train with North Country sleepers for connecting trains.
61 & 62	Montreal Limited	#61 was formerly #65 - Pullman sleepers only between Montreal and New York via D&H. Later Rutland cars were also carried.
63	Genesee	Another Indian name, this one was the heavyweight for New York to Buffalo sleepers. During World War II when sleepers were prohibited between New York and Buffalo this operated with later afternoon departure with all reserved seats in coaches and parlors.
63 & 64	Water Level Limited	Post-war late p.m. departure between New York and Chicago, sleepers and coaches.
65 & 66	Advance Commodore Vanderbilt	17-hour mid-afternoon Pullman and coach train between New York and Chicago was #37 westbound for a short time. Inaugurated 1940 eastbound only as the "Grand Central", renamed and put in service both directions in 1941, initially Pullmans Only.
67 & 68	Commodore Vanderbilt	Inaugurated Sept. 1929 as a later relief for Century on 20-hour schedule. Extra-fare and extra plush and second only to the Century on the system as a choice for New York-Chicago passengers.
71 & 72	Mount Royal	#71 later #145. This was the overnight New York-Montreal via Rutland RR train with sleepers and coaches.
75 & 76	Mercury	Inaugurated 1936 between Detroit and Cleveland with rebuilt commuter cars and later when more rebuilt equipment available was extended to Chicago in 1939.
80	Maumee	Overnight Chicago to Cleveland with varied equipment for Buffalo and Pittsburgh via connecting trains.
81 & 82	Genesee	Overnighter between New York and Buffalo post-war successor to #63 after going back to carrying sleepers.
82	Ontarian	Overnight sleepers only Toronto and Buffalo to New York. Eastbound counterpart of Toronto Limited.
85	Detroit Express	Daytime Pittsburgh to Detroit train featuring parlor observation. Depression casualty.
86	Pittsburgh Express	Counterpart to #86.
87	Lake Cities Special	Overnighter with sleepers and coaches Pittsburgh to Detroit.
88	Pittsburgh Special	Counterpart to #87.
89	Forest City	Overnight Pullman Cars Only Cleveland to Chicago.
90	Forest City	Originally overnight sleepers only Chicago to Cleveland, later extended east as far as New York with coaches as well. Sometime later renamed "Chicagoan" and sleepers Chicago to Cleveland carried in #290, a new "Forest City".
96	New York Special	Later known as "New York Express". Prior to 1941 streamlining of Empire train number #50 did not operate as such on Sundays. This train carried Empire's equipment and operated on almost same, but slightly slower, schedule.
96	Advance Empire State Express	After World War II this Buffalo to New York train carried pre-streamlined Empire's cars off Adirondack Div. handled in #90 during war.
97 & 98	Paul Revere	During period New England States operated Pullman only this was the Boston and Chicago coach train usually combined with some main line NYC train west of Cleveland or Buffalo. Occasionally carried sleepers in combination with other B&A trains.
135	Seneca	One of the many trains bearing this name at one time or another (like the Cayuga) this was a post-World War II overnight New York to Buffalo with the Rochester, Syracuse, Oswego, Utica sleepers and Buffalo coaches.
138	Up State Special	Short lived eastbound counterpart of #167 during brief period ex-Mercury equipment was the makeup or part thereof, late '40's.
140	North Star	Post WW II early morning arrival in New York with sleepers off Adirondack Div. formerly in #44 and other trains.
142	Prairie State	Late Cleveland departure for New York with Buffalo, Toronto, Rochester and New York sleepers. At various periods shortened run.

143 & 144	Laurentian	Daytime (mostly summer only) train with D&H and Rutland at times coaches and parlors New York to Montreal.
163	Champlain	Summer only morning train augmenting Laurentian with D&H parlors and coaches for North Creek, Lake George, Saratoga Springs.
167	Up State Special	For a short time was operated as #57 and combined with #67 between New York and Albany this was the late afternoon train from New York to Syracuse. After Mercury got new equipment in 1948 one set of older cars saw service on the "Upstate", sometimes numbered #367.
342	Detroit Special	Overnighter Chicago to Detroit with coaches and sleepers.
345	Valley Express	Westbound counterpart to above.
358	Canadian & Niagara	Overnight Chicago to Buffalo and Toronto via M.C.R.R.
405	Sycamore	Late day flyer Cincinnati to Chicago. Better scheduled time than J.W. Riley.
416	Cincinnati Special	Opposite number of #405.
427	Gateway	Cleveland to Cincinnati overnighter.

The foregoing by no means pretends to be an all-inclusive list of "name" trains operated during the "glory days" and should not be construed as such. By and large, though, these are the trains of the "Hudson" era. While many operated also prior to the advent of the 4-6-4's there were others that were ushered in with them, indeed some were only possible because of the J-1's superior performances. Anyway, here they were - the "Great Steel Fleet".

Pencil sketch by the author, about 1948.

New York Central

HEAD END

New York Central

54′ 2½″ express baggage cars (9200-9399), built for the War Department, 1946, by Pullman Standard as troop sleepers. Converted at Despatch shops 1947-48.

50′ milk car. Plenty of these around. Between 1914 and 1931, 225 were built by M.D.T. Company of Rochester, New York, (This was built in 1928).

264

...of twenty 70' Baggage Cars built for the ...Four by American Car and Foundry in...

Above: One of fifty 60'6" Steel Baggage Cars (3311-3360) built by A.C.&F. (American Car & Foundry) at Berwick, Pa. in 1924.
Below: Baggage Mail 3928 was built by Standard Steel Car Co. in 1926 in a lot of thirty two. (3923-3954).

New York Central

New York Central

One of fourteen Horse Cars (5600-5613) built by A.C.&F. Berwick, Pa. in 1928. Car is 70' long and only one end had the gate doors. Last seven were converted in 1958 to Baggage Cars.

One of seven (9061-9067) 75' Baggage Cars built at Beech Grove in 1942. This car was originally built as Big Four passenger coach by A.C.&F. in 1930. Colors were Black roof and trucks, olive drab car body and deep yellow stripes and lettering. A color scheme used for a while by N.Y.C. in the early 40's.

New York Central

HEAD END

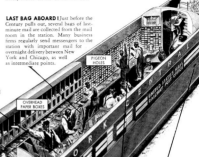

New York Central ad of 1944 showing the inner workings of an RPO car.
Interesting, that mail service for distances under 1,000 miles was better in 1944 than 1974. But, we must have progress and justify our air age expenditures.

One of four (4907-4910) Postal cars built by A.C.&F. in 1947. Don't know if car was intended for "Century" but it certainly saw service on same.

New York Central

One of two (5014-5015) 70′ Mail R.P.O. cars built for the new 1948 20th Century Limited.

New York Central

267

Standard 70' steel passenger baggage. Built by Pressed Steel Car Company, McKees Rocks, Pa., 1924. Seats 48 and was never air conditioned. Weight was about 70 tons.

Standard 70' steel coach built by Pressed Steel Car Company, McKees Rocks, Pa., 1925. Later air conditioned and in service today (1974). 70' measurement does not include vestibules, so actual length over coupler was about 79'.

70 foot (actually 79') suburban coach, one of a lot of fifty, built by Osgood-Bradley in 1925 for the Boston & Albany. Car is similar to those built later for Putnam Div. and rebuilt for "Mercury". See following page.

70' coach built for Boston & Albany by Pullman Car & Mfg. Corp., Pullman, Ill. 1928. Built with 88 seats.

2640 was in one of three lots of new 84'6" coaches ordered in 1941 for luxury coach service. Ninety five cars were built by Pullman (1941, 2600-2644), A.C.&F. (1941-42, 2645-2669) and Pressed Steel Car Company (1942, 2670-2694). All had 56 seats, air conditioning and colors were olive drab with yellow strips. Later painted two tone gray. Many are still in service.

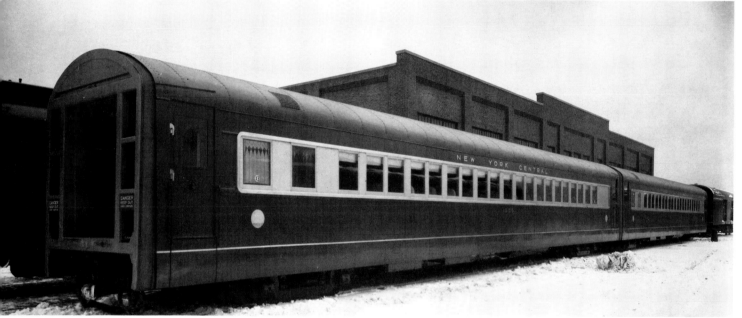

New York Central

Mercury Car 1005 rebuilt at Beech Grove in 1936 from suburban coach 2407 which was originally built by Osgood-Bradley in 1927 for Putnam Division service. Twenty of these became Mercury cars between 1936-39, all at Beech Grove. See third picture opposite page.

COACHES

Passenger boarding New York Central coaches at Linndale, Ohio. Train is #37, Prairie State.

Jack McGroarty

Ed Nowak - New York Cen

THE PACEMAKER

When the "Pacemaker" was hurriedly inaugurated on July 28, 1939 to compete with Pennsy "Trailblazer" they had to temporarily use two converted "Century" observation cars in the "Valley" series. They were Catskill Valley and Seneca Valley, which became 2598-2599. These cars were painted two tone gray and remained in service until replaced by closed ones which were rebuilt lounge-observations off the old Day Coach Deluxe. Cars 53, 56 were converted at Beech Grove 1940.

This car was being readied for westbound run #3 "Pacemaker" at Mott Haven, August 9, 1939. This sign was put on at Grand Central.

"Pacemaker" westbound July 14, 1940, Manitou, N.Y. Obs. 2599 is ex-Pullman "Seneca Valley" (built 1930) and used on this train from July 28, 1939 to September 14, 1940.

Edward L. May

New York Central

70' coach, originally built with 85 seats in 1920, shown here after conversion to 52 seats, smoking room and Frigidaire air conditioning. Weight was 143,100 lbs.

Diner 427 was originally from lot 2042, nos. 416-435 built by Pullman in 1927. Car is shown here February 21, 1934 after the installation of mechanized air conditioning. Entire lot later renumbered 627-646. Car weighed 184,000 lbs.

DINERS

Left and right side view of standard 1925 New York Central diner. 391 and 392 were lot 978 and represented NYC nos. 391-400. Identical to these and also built by Pullman were Big Four diners 1129-1138 and Michigan Centrals 138 and 139.

391 and 392 later became 582 and 583. Diner 582 later became a diner lounge with 22 dining seats and 14 lounge seats. As built, they had 36 dining seats only.

P&LE #1, only diner on the Pittsburgh & Lake Erie. Car was actually diner-lounge with 18 dining seats and 12 lounge seats. Car was built by Pullman in 1925 and weighed 175,100 lbs. No. 1 is shown here after air conditioning in the mid 1930's.

New York Central

This car and the car ahead are companion full kitchen lounge and full diner. Built by Budd in 1947.

Always a familiar sight, a cook, steward or conductor lookin' over the passengers at every stop or slow speed.

Al Staufer collection

NEW YORK CENTRAL'S ORIGINAL DE LUXE COACH TRAINS

In the 1920's much of the overnight and long-haul traffic on the New York Central Lines was luxury Pullman travel. Few trains afforded decent coach travel between major cities. There was #3 "Chicago Express", a mere 23 hours and 55 minutes, $4.80 extra fare and featuring the standard 85 straight back coach seats, a favorite(?) of the era. Then there was #5 "Mohawk", a comparatively fast 22-hour train at $7.00 extra fare. Mid-day saw the Westerner #7, only 26 hours with no extra fare and followed in early evening by #23 "Western Express", another 26-hour, no extra fare job.

It took the depression and the inroads of bus and private car competition to change all this and the result, somewhat belatedly, was fancy coach equipment on the fast limiteds in the mid-'30's and then, lastly, followed by exclusive coach luxury trains in the years just prior to World War II.

However, almost forgotten were the forerunners of these all-coach streamliners inaugurated in 1928 and 1929 between some main cities on the New York Central Lines and covering their runs entirely in daytime hours. There was the train between New York and Buffalo, another between Cincinnati and Detroit and the third that ran between Chicago and Buffalo via Detroit and the M.C.R.R. and Niagara Falls.

The first train inaugurated on June 24, 1928 was the Day Coach DeLuxe between New York and Buffalo and consisted of 82 seat coaches (bucket type), dining car, combo smoker and open end observation coach with 54 movable wicker chairs. The inside of the coaches were decorated in brown, walnut grain finish and brown carpet. There were porters in attendance and the train covered the 438 miles in 10 hours and 20 minutes while making 18 intermediate stops. During the first summer the westbound train (#1) averaged 347 passengers and the eastbound train (#2) averaged 371 passengers. The following winter, surprisingly enough, saw only a slight letdown with 353 average westbound passengers and 337 average eastbound customers. Also, it was a further pleasant surprise to note that there was no visible drop in passengers on the train that traversed the same route on a faster and slightly earlier schedule, the Empire State Express. The Day Coach continued in operation, in one fashion or another, for many years. First, it extended the coach run to Cleveland, added a Cleveland parlor car, a Chicago sleeper handled in other trains west of Buffalo and, for a short period, was cut to operate only New York to Syracuse and its name was changed to Cayuga. During winter months it handled the equipment of the D&H Laurentian, the daytime NY-Montreal train, between New York and Albany. Finally, after the Empire was streamlined late in

1941, the Cayuga carried the Adirondack Division cars between New York and Utica formerly part of the Empire consist. This operated for the last decade until through Adirondack cars were abolished. By this time it was Train #55, #1 long before having been given to the Pacemaker, which for a short time was #3. The fine performance, maintaining a good schedule, of the early Day Coach De Luxe was due in no small measure to the advent of the 5200 series engines. K-3q Pacifics might not have been practicable.

A year after the Day Coach was inaugurated, April 28, 1929, two other exclusive coach trains appeared. The "Motor Queen" was placed in service between Cincinnati and Detroit, its equipment sporting an exterior of rich brown with stripes of fawn along the middle of the sides and around under casements. A coach smoker combo, cafe lounge, bucket seat coaches and observation coach made it a counterpart of the east's Day Coach. Leaving Cincinnati at 3:30 p.m. it arrived in Detroit at 9:40 p.m. Its opposite number left Detroit 3:05 p.m. and pulled into Cincinnati at 9:15 p.m. It failed by a wide margin to emulate the success of the Day Coach, however, and was withdrawn December 7th, the same year.

Also in 1929, "The Niagara Falls DeLuxe Special" started operation between Chicago and Buffalo via MC RR and Niagara Falls. It carried the same type of equipment as its brethren and the identical color scheme as the "Motor Queen". Eastbound it departed Chicago at 8 a.m. and arrived Buffalo 8:30 p.m. Its westbound run left Buffalo 10 a.m. and arrived the Windy City 8:30 p.m. This train proved more successful than the "Motor Queen" and as of 6/7/30 was still operating.

Newly acquired Michigan Central Hudsons likely handled the Niagara Falls DeLuxe Special but the relatively short Motor Queen was probably hauled by K-5 Pacifics.

DE LUXE DAY COACH

"Pacemaker", Chicago, Ill. October 7, 1940.
Closed observations cars 53 and 56 replaced open end platform cars 2598 and 2599 on September 14, 1940. Train was sort of a khaki brown with yellow striping and red ovals above car numbers. These reclining seat deluxe coaches were rebuilds, but replaced by 2600 series, 56 seat cars in 1941-42. All this equipment ultimately was replaced in 1947-48 by Budd stainless steel 2900 series coaches and observation cars 48-51.

Lee A. Hastman collection

Beautiful rich brown and fawn cars of short lived Motor Queen.

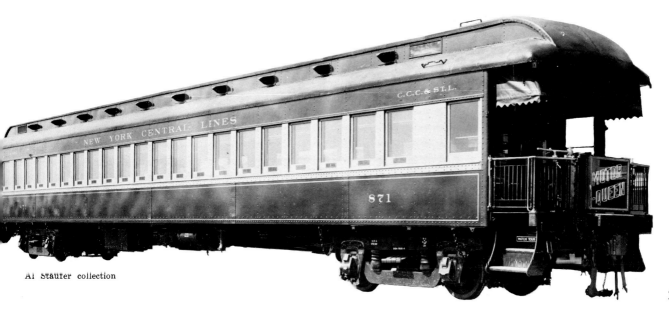

Al Stauffer collection

Big Four Deluxe, one of two, Cafe Lounge Cars, 1160-1161. Converted at Beech Grove, Ind., 1929. We don't know what 1161 was rebuilt from but truss rods would indicate it predates World War I.

DE LUXE DAY COACH

One of ten M.C. coaches (426-435) built by Pullman, 1927, as lot 2059 which included twenty-five 70′ coaches in all (415-439).

Rebuilt at West Albany 1929 for service in "Niagara Falls DeLuxe Special", which operated between Chicago and Buffalo via the Michigan Central.

All were later air conditioned with 58 reclining seats.

745-746, and 747 were converted from coaches in 1928 and 1929. The philosophy of the time was such that a train just wasn't complete unless tailed by an open platform observation car.

New York Central

VAN TWILLER, baggage-club car for "Century" contained buffet, baggage and barber. Pullman, 1930.

SARAH BERNHARDT, Pullman 1927, Parlor, 30 chair, drawing room, assigned Michigan Central "Twilight Limited".

GAIL BORDEN, old "EAST BUFFALO" renamed for president of Borden Milk. Trucks are commonwealth straight equalized instead of the usual bottom equalized type. All bearings of this period were brass.

CHURCHVILLE, Pullman 1930. 12 sections and drawing room. A standard car on all NYC overnight runs.

ROSA BONHEUR, Pullman, 1927, 34 seat parlor for MC's "Twilight Limited". This car was one of 47 purchased from Pullman in 1942 and converted to reclining seat coaches at Beech Grove.

CENTSTAR, 8 sections, 1 drawing room, 2 compartments. Regular NYC equipment on Limiteds in the early 30's.

POINT CUTHBERT, Pullman, 1926, 10 sections, 2 drawing rooms. Sections were made up into the old traditional upper and lower berths.

CAMP MEIGS, Pullman, 1921, 10 sections, 1 drawing room, 2 compartments, 1928 Century was made up with two cars of this type, NY-Chicago, and Boston-Chicago.

JENNY LIND, Pullman, 1927, 28 seat parlor car assigned to Michigan Centrals "Twilight Limited".

SENECA VALLEY, Pullman, 1930, drawing room, single bedroom, observation. Real NYC deluxe trademark for "Century" and "Southwestern Limited". Last open observation built before streamlining. This car later converted 1939 for use on "Pacemaker".

PULLMAN OBSERVATION

PULLMAN

DETROIT CLUB, Pullman, 1930, 8 sections, buffet, lounge, solarium, observation. Assigned to Michigan Central's "Motor City Special". Car has purity of functional charm, just plain beautiful. Roof is black, Sides are Pullman Green, lettering gold, trucks black (sometimes Pullman Green) and window sash is painted either bronze or aluminum.

APTHORPE HOUSE, Pullman, 1930. 13 double bedroom car for "Twentieth Century Limited" only in the early 1930's. Color same as above car.

COACH

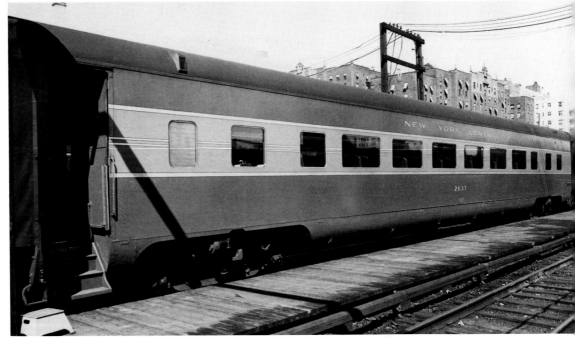

New York Central

The original 1938 streamlined "Century" color scheme (see following page) with the wide stripes down the middle of the windows was just not right and most instinctively knew it. Early in 1940 the railroad began experimenting with different colors and arrangements.

Above is coach in experimental grays and thin stripes. Colors on the car just ahead were finally selected as second streamline motif.

Below is "Cascade Vale", one of the two cars painted in experimental shades of green (other was Imperial Palace). Each car was painted light and dark green with aluminum stripes which were outlined in black. Each car had one half of the roof painted medium green and the other black.

New York Central

GREEN

 All steel business car, Pullman, 1930. Car No. 1 was one of the last of the golden age of individuality. All class and it shows it too. Interior contained kitchen, dining room, 4 big staterooms and observation room. No lightweight, it tipped the scales at 204,300 lbs.

PRIVATE

Private car FRIENDSHIP owned by newspaper publishing magnate, Paul Block.

Color of post war smooth side streamliners was tasteful two tone gray with white stripes edged in black. Lettering was also white.

 Al Staufer collection

New York Central

Brand new streamlined IMPERIAL FOUNTAIN, 4 compartments, 4 double bedrooms, 2 drawing rooms. Body sides were two tone gray with white stripes through windows, at top and bottom of car and lettering. Band above and below window was blue. All stripes in middle area were outlined in thin black lines as was the car name.

It doesn't look too bad here, brand new, and with all shades pulled down but it was over-all just too darned "busy" design-wise. It lasted about two years and all cars were repainted as per middle picture page 282. The 1948 colors (preceding bottom page) were the best.

New York Central

"Century" in original livery, westbound just east of Peekskill.

New York Central

284

It's all so perfect and harmonious. Functionalism ruled in the design of the engine, catenary, and buildings, but amazing how it all holds together so well.

"CUT" (Cleveland Union Terminal) motor 208 pulling 9 car #50, eastbound "Empire State Express". 216 is switching.

We admit complete bias on this scene. Photographed by Robert Doeddener.

One of the two 85′ mail baggage built for the "Empire State Express" by Budd Co. in 1941. This is "Alonzo B. Cornell"; the other is "John A. Dix" shown below.

EMPIRE STATE EXPRESS

One of two 85′ tavern, lounge, baggage for "Empire". Companion to "Grover Cleveland" is "Martin Van Buren".

Al Staufer collection

Four 85' diners were built by Budd for the Empire. Names were: John Jay, Horatio Seymour, George Clinton and DeWitt Clinton.

BUDD

New York Central

32 cars were ordered for the trains. Six were coaches numbered 2564-2569, the other 26 were named for New York State Governors, four of whom became presidents.

Two tavern lounge observations were built for the train. This one was named "Theodore Roosevelt" the other after that other Roosevelt.

Richard J. Cook

CLEVELAND

No railroad that we know of had so many differently colored passenger cars at one time. They had Pullman green, stainless steel, stainless steel with black roof, two tone gray, and coach green. Intentions were never to run these all mixed up in one train but that's the way it was in 1951.

Hudson has just delivered #59 to Collinwood where C.U.T. electric 213 rushes train to Cleveland's terminal. Photo by Bob Boeddener.

Al Staufer collection

TARRYTOWN HARBOR, one of thirty one single roomette cars received from Budd in 1949. Above, as built with full width diaphragms and Pullman on the letterboard. Right: same car some years later with NYC on middle letterhead and outerskirts of diaphragm removed.

Stainless steel coach with serif lettering. One of two (2560-2561) 52 seat coaches built by Budd in 1938. 2562 followed in 1939 and 2563 in 1940.

BUDD

PLUM BROOK, built by Budd not Pullman, in 1949. Car is 85′ 5 drawing room, lounge observation. One of three.

No. 48, tavern, lounge, observation built by Budd in 1948 for service on Pacemaker and probably James Whitcomb Riley. Here was the fun car to ride. And railroad cocktails are the 2 oz. variety. Maybe again someday.

FROM THE MEN

New York Central

Bob Butterfield

The most famous New York Central engineer of all times, including Charlie Hogan and his renown run with No. 999, was Robert E. Butterfield. Fame is an elusive ingredient, sought after by so many but caught by so few. It takes desire and ability, and probably in that order. Bob Butterfield had the ability and circumstance, being senior engineer on the Hudson Division in the Golden Years; he also had the desire. His name became synonymous with the train he drove, the "Twentieth Century Limited". He loved his job with its resulting publicity and fame. He looked and lived the part. On his days off he would eagerly speak to railfan groups, appear on radio programs, or pose for publicity and endorsement photographs.

Few are aware that during the years 1923-1929, Lionel Corporation did not offer a single steam style electric train. All were electric, influenced in great part by the almost complete electrification around New York City. In 1930 they introduced a couple of steam models but the big push was timed for 1931. How did they choose to publicise the re-entry into

Here he is, the most famous engineer on the mighty New York Central with his fireman in the cab of their favorite type locomotive, a J1 Hudson.
We doubt if any notable person of the times in the entire USA didn't at sometime or another ride behind Bob and his thundering steed. Who knows who is back in those Pullmans this very instant? Maybe the New York Yankees with Ruth, Gehrig, Combs. Meusel, Lazzeri, Pennock — off to conquer again.

steam? How else but with Robert E. Butterfield. The 1931 catalog cover shows Bob holding newly introduced 400E to his two grandsons, Richard and Robert E. the 3rd, standing in front of the drivers of a J1b. Caption on cover was "Just Like Mine" says Bob Butterfield, engineer of the "20th Century Limited". The model he was holding bore little resemblance to the magnificent machines he drove. It doesn't really matter all that much in toy trains anyway, it's the spirit that counts.

Physically, Bob was a short muscular type; sort of a James Cagney with a pug nose. He claimed 5'6" height but we suspect that was the shoes and standing on a 2" plaform. He sat tall where it mattered — in the right hand seat of a J1 Hudson. And he didn't drink, smoke, or play cards either. Really!

Born in Manhattan, April 19, 1867, son of a Hudson River R.R engineer, signed on at 16 as an "oil boy" at the NYC & HR's 72nd St. roundhouse in New York City. He became a freight engineer in

1890 and passenger in 1899. In Oct. 1904, running a late mail train, in the 3.51 miles between Croton and Ossining, he hit 105 m.p.h. He handled the "Century" for 20 years between Harmon and Albany. Last run was May 5, 1938 eastbound from Albany to Harmon on Train #22 "Lake Shore Limited", thus ending 54 years of service.

Engineers got mileage per weight of locomotive on driving wheels with different rate for freight or passenger. Runs were chosen by seniority; Bob's paid 6.96 cents per mile, or about $21.00 for a round trip from Harmon to Albany and Back. Not bad for 1931. Rules limited him to 4,800 miles a month so he laid off every third day.

Average run was something like this: arrives early to oil and check his engine. Leaves Harmon at 3:35 P.M. with the Twentieth Century. Gets to Albany at 5:38. Makes himself a cup of coffee in the locker room. At 6:35 P.M. drives the Empire State Express back to Harmon. Rides in local to within 12 minutes of his home in Ossining. Has snack (waiting in icebox prepared for him by Mrs.) and in bed by 11:30.

Has three boys, two girls, three grand children (1931). Loves to garden and favorite song is let "Let Me Call You Sweetheart".

Doesn't mind too much not having personal locomotive since the "Century" always has the latest and best available. All notables want to ride with him especially aviators. "It gives them more of a kick than flying."

"I think my job is the next thing to getting a check for doing nothing."

And who are we to argue with that.

Edward L. May collection

P. J. Beaver, engineer of Pennsylvania's "Broadway Limited" and Bob Butterfield, engineer of New York Central's "Twentieth Century Limited".

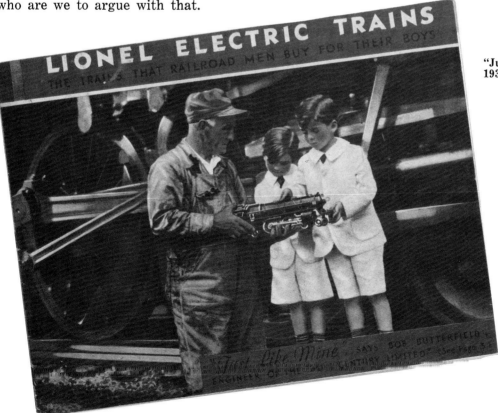

"Just Like Mine" says Bob. 1931 Lionel catalog.

My plans to publish a book on the New York Central Hudson type locomotive dates back about 20 years. Ten years ago (1963) it occurred to me that if I was ever to gather living evidence, now was the time. The Hudsons had just about had it at the close of 1955 and considering the railroad's seniority system, the matter was urgent. At that time (1963) too many former Hudson drivers were in their seventies.

The Brotherhood of Locomotive Engineers assisted me by publicizing my needs in their paper "Locomotive Engineers." We requested anything the former engineer cared to say — unusual experiences, likes, dislikes, etc. Their response, and even the response of non-rail employees, was most generous.

We present some here as "pure" as possible with no attempt at re-writing or "coloring" them up. In most cases, however, we get to the very "heart" of what they had to say and only delete opening or non-pertinent comments.

FROM THE MEN

From C. A. Peterson, Syracuse, N.Y.

"In the summer of 1935 I was firing train #50, the Empire State Express for William (Billy) Lynch (deceased) and at Boliver Crossing, about 15 miles east of Syracuse, Mohawk Division, while traveling about 75 MPH we collided with a ten-wheel truck loaded with 10 tons of gravel. The locomotive's whistle had and was blowing the regulation two long, one short and one long blast (as witnesses later testified) but the 21 year old driver of the truck claimed that he did not hear the whistle. He saw the train bearing down on him just as he got to the tracks, and being unable to stop the heavy truck, he unloaded a second or two from the track and the truck kept on rolling and we hit it broadside tearing the two air pumps and air pipes loose from the pilot of locomotive 5273 (the one shown in your picture) and of course causing the air brakes to apply in emergency, and we came to a stop about one half mile east of the accident with flat wheels on 12 of the 15 cars we had in the train. Gravel was packed in around the air pumps and under the smoke box so tight that it was necessary to use crow bars and pick-axes to later pry the gravel loose. Also gravel had torn out the two front windows of the cab, and there was about two or three inches of gravel on the deck of the cab and all Billy Lynch received was a slight cut on one hand and all I received was a bruise on one ankle and a bump on my forehead. The truck body landed on the top of the boiler and the frame rode the rails under the pilot and against the front wheels of the pony truck until we stopped, and luckily we did not derail as before we came to a stop we passed through Chittenango Creek bridge and the girders of that bridge still show the scars of where that truck frame hit.

"About one hour later we were pulled back to Kirkville where we received a fresh locomotive and proceeded on to Utica at 20 MPH where the passengers and mail were transferred to cars without flat wheels.

"In my opinion the 5200 class were snappier than the 5400s were in getting away at the start but once under way the 5400s were smoother in operation. The 5300's were just a so-so locomotive.

"I went firing in 1911, promoted in 1916, and back and forth until my last year of firing was 1936. I retired on August 30th, 1957 at age 65 and my wife and I have been having a ball ever since."

From E. J. Muhn, Waterville, Ohio

"I am now working as a Hostler on the Wabash, However in 1939 thru 1942 I worked on the NYC as an outside Hostler Helper on the Passenger side of the roundhouse at Airline Junction, Toledo, Ohio.

"The 5454, known to us at that time as the "Covered Wagon" was on the 20th Century Run, West. We used to take her to the Depot at Toledo and return the cutoff Eng. usually a 5400 class Eng. As you probably know she was roller bearing throughout. Including the main rod and eccentric ends. On level track two men could move her by pushing. Other Engs. we had as l recall was the 5450 with "disk" wheels, but not roller bearing like the 5454.

"As far as bugs in the Engine only Honycombing of the small flues near the crown sheet, which caused the Eng. to not steam properly."

From Bob LeMassena, Denver, Colo.

"My earliest recollections of them were at Springfield on the B & A. When an eastbound train pulled out, up the hill, the 4-6-4 would bark slowly, almost majestically, as it tackled the grade. Then, after 15 cars went by, an 0-8-0 came bouncing along, shoving against the rear-end and sounding like a Shay at full-speed. It was an amusing comparison, and I enjoyed it on several occasions.

During the War, I saw them in Chicago, and I remember one railfan who was on the narrow platform at Grand Island Crossing when two Hudsons passed simultaneously, both at high speed. He said that his handprints are permanently engraved in the lamp-post to which he had hung during this soul-shattering episode.

In post-War days, I took the Interstate Express from Chicago, behind a Hudson which wasted no time en-route. As we passed Englewood, I noticed a pair of them just backing out of the engine terminal for La Salle St. Station to get the mail train which followed the Interstate. You can imagine my surprise when these same two engines pulled into Toledo right alongside of us!"

From Raymond K. Smith, Lansing, Mich.

"I had the pleasure of firing one of these engines in a branch line passenger run in 1955 on trains 351 and 352.

"Our regular engine was J3 5429. It was a pure delight to fire this engine. While we had rather light trains, seven to eight coaches, there were places that we could test the true performance of the engine. One such place was Owosso, Mich. where southbound trains climbed a steady grade for about three miles out of town. We planned to test the time from stand still to sixty using standard stop watch.

"I allowed the water to just show in the glass and prepared a hand fire while doing station work.

"When we received the highball, the engineer, H. Brazee, started the watch and opened the throttle. The engine slipped once but otherwise worked at full power. In exactly 90 seconds the speed recorder crossed sixty, the track speed. It was interesting to note that on an L4 good running condition with the same train required 2 min. to obtain the same speed.

"Later, with steam-power retired, we tried this test with a single G.M.G.P.7 Passenger engine. Unfortunately we never completed the test as the engine never reached 60 till we passed the next town!"

From Hugh P. Welch, Rochester, N.Y.

"I am writing in regards to one engine, the 5413 — in other words, the numbers add up to 13 which is supposed to be unlucky. I was firing at the time but home on leave from the Army 1945. The 5413 was on #6 Buffalo to Syracuse. Coming into Rochester the train jumped the track and the engine plunged into a house at 11:30 P.M. into a man's bedroom who died of a heart attack. The engineer on 5413 was killed. The cause of the wreck was never known however the company blamed the engineer for too much speed. The engineer was on this job regular & knew every inch of rail. His fireman was hurt very bad & never went on the road but stayed in yard service.

This engine was repaired & saw service again where she stripped herself — tore off her main rods & did a lot of damage.

Another time she was in Rochester engine house for service where she ran away through switches and did a lot of damage. I wonder if her number might have been the trouble. 5413 = 13.

I am an engineer now and look back at those wonderful engines and still think the 5200's were the best steaming & easiest firing engines of all time."

From James L. Costello, Kellys Island, Ohio.

"I fired one of the first ones to come through Buffalo on train #19. The snow was around three feet deep. It was 19° below zero. It had a Standard Stoker so you can picture what conditions were that morning.

The engine I liked to fire best was the 5449, one of the "covered wagons". She had thermostat in back of the fireman's seat which gave you the degrees of heat in the four corners of the firebox.

When they were right they steamed good. In those days of firing it was like getting manna from heaven when the stokers came in.

I was with the old Lake Shore and NYC for 49 years & 6 months."

From Paul Strayer, River Forest, Ill.

"Until the year 1931 I had never seen a locomotive of the so-called Hudson type. My work of artist-painter and illustrator — much of it along industrial lines, together with a love of the steam locomotive dating from my childhood days, had familiarized me with Atlantics and Pacifics and Mountains and many of the freight pullers, but the new Hudson was a thrill I had missed.

I shall never forget my first impression of the magnificent locomotive as it backed into the New York Central Station in Chicago to be coupled to the fourteen car train of the Twentieth Century Limited.

Of course the first thing that impressed me was the unique four wheel trailing truck; but then an awareness of perfect balance transcended this interest. The height of the stack; the streamlining of it and the forward steam exhaust and the sand and steam domes and encasing of the piping in front of the cab and the compressors within their shields and the pilot and the front coupler so snugly and smoothly resting in its recess. The magnificent driver assembly — how perfectly the drivers were proportioned to the complete ensemble. How strange, I later thought, when I familiarized myself with their dimensions that an inch — a single inch — added or subtracted from that of seventy nine would have missed it.

The great locomotive was coupled so gently to

its train that an egg would hardly have been broken in the process. And then I walked around it! From side to front to side. No view of the splendid engine that was not completely eye-filling — completely balanced. I had never before seen any aggregation of mechanical parts combined with immense power and with it all a beauty unsurpassed in mechanics. Another of the — to me — most beautiful eye-comforts was before me. May I list them here? A Doric temple, a square rigged ship under full sail, on a broad reach; a thoroughbred horse under a blanket and now — the ultimate in efficiency and mechanical beauty — the Hudson — New Yerk Central — 4-6-4.

Later, through the courtesy of the head of the Public Relations Department of the New York Central Railroad, I was privileged to ride in the cab of the great Hudson from Chicago to Elkhart, Indiana. I shall never forget my trepidation as I looked down from a height of some eleven or twelve feet and thought of a mass of some three hundred tons of steel hurtling along the ribbon-rails at a speed of some eighty miles an hour. I remember the fireman looked at me quizzically and said, "don't worry; if anything happens you won't know anything about it." But I considered the forth-coming experience well worth the possible apprehension.

The data gleaned from this trip was later used in developing a painting of the Twentieth Century Limited departing from the LaSalle St., station in Chicago. It occupied the center, north wall of the New York Central exhibit of the Century of Progress Exposition of Chicago of 1933."

From W. H. Rossiter, West Hill, Ontario, Canada.

"Going back to the old days at John St. Roundhouse in Toronto. I remember well those hectic Thursday evenings just before the Good Friday holiday weekends. The NYC would dispatch from its East Buffalo engine house pool, as many as 5 Hudsons, running light to Toronto to handle the four or five sections of CPR #821. This was the heavy sleeping car train to New York City and other American points. This was a common occurence for years. The Hudsons that were not in regular Canadian service gave some headaches to the roundhouse staff. They were not equipped with marker lamps as this practice had been discontinued on the Central. There would be a mad rush to apply electric markers to the pilot beams of these engines. I presume the equipment was later returned to the CPR (Canadian Pacific Railroad) at Toronto.

I remember 5214 was laid up for a week at Toronto awaiting parts for its valve gear. The CPR didn't stock parts for them. They had to be sent over from Buffalo.

The reason for sending all the Hudsons to Toronto for Good Friday weekend was because the CPR did not have enough Power, fitted with ATC (Automatic Train Control) to run into Buffalo. There were only 4 CPR engines with ATC for International service. The T.H.&B (Toronto, Hamilton & Buffalo) also had only 4 thus equipped.

THE NYC Hudsons had gadgets on them which were not found on CPR engines. Low water alarm, pyrometer, valve pilot, etc.

I remember one of the CPR engineers who was on the Toronto-Hamilton run, saying you had to have a university degree to run them. Most of the hoggers liked their smooth riding qualities."

From John Xifus, Long Island City, N.Y.

I am employed in the engine service on the New York Central Hudson Division and I have fired the 5200's for many years while they were in service on the Hudson division.

It was a wonderful engine to fire. When these engines first arrived on the N.Y.C. they were equipped with the Duplex type stokers which fed the coal from the left side and the right side of the firebox. Later they were all changed to either the H.T. type stoker or the B.K. type. I preferred the H.T. stoker for with that, you could do almost anything with the coal. I cannot say much more for I was on the fireman's roster and a good deal of the time I fired freight. The 5200's were used on freight many times, as the Troy freight always had a 5200 out of Harmon. After it terminated its run at Troy, it would be Yd' or backed down to Rensselear where they could use the engine on a passenger train, as Rensselaer was a passenger roundhouse for Albany terminal and Troy. Many times I fired the Troy freight with a Hudson type engine and I recall one time pulling out of Poughkeepsie, N.Y. with more than a hundred cars and doing a very nice job of it.

From Tom Mulaniff, Cheektowaga, N.Y.

"I happened to be one of ones who fired them but never had the fortune to run, only under the guidance of the hogger, much to my great sorrow. In fact I never ran a steamer on my own, only over in India when in the service. But I fired plenty of them, also the "Mohawks" and "Niagaras". I have one experience to tell you that stands out in my mind and I'll proceed to do so.

Before I entered the service I got called for a passenger run on the Falls Branch. This branch runs from Buffalo to Niagara Falls and Suspension Bridge, N.Y. As a general rule we made two round trips from Buffalo to the Bridge and return. The only one trippers we made were on extra sections and troop trains out of Fort Niagara. On this particular trip we were returning from Suspension

Bridge with #248 on the last trip. This train used to connect with #8, "The Wolverine" at Buffalo. We had four cars, a baggage car, two coaches and a N.Y. sleeper for #8 that was picked up at the Niagara Falls depot. This sleeper had to make #8. On the headend of this train was the 5408, a J-3 Hudson. My engineer was a real ballast scorcher from way back. When he got a few brownies under his belt, he thought he had the "Century" under his command. Now bear in mind that it is only 28 miles from the Bridge depot to Central Terminal in Buffalo. We left Suspension Bridge 26 minutes behind the carded time. We stopped at the Falls to pick up the car for #8 and highballed for Buffalo, and I do mean highballed. We stopped at North Tonawanda, Black Rock, The Terrace and into Central Terminal.

With the three stops mentioned and the one at the Falls, which took a little extra time, as the air had to be tried, you can imagine that to go to Buffalo and arrive on time had to take some high wheeled running. There was, of course, a little extra time given because of picking up the sleeper at the Falls. I cannot remember the exact running time or the schedule as it happened so long ago and like a darn fool, I never retained any of the time cards from those days. As far as I can remember though, the running time was around 55 minutes. Let me tell you that the 5408 really kicked up its heels that night. The top speed on the branch was 60 MPH but that night the speed was thrown right out the cab window. It was between 70 & 75 on the straight away and on one curve east of Tonawanda station, the limit was 40. We took that at 60 and I thought all my corn was popped when we hit that curve. The engine held on and straightened up although it was touch and go for a few moments. That was the only bad ride of the whole trip as the rest of the track was fairly tangent. I had trouble keeping the engine hot and supplying the boiler with water with only four cars. She just wouldn't do business. When we arrived at Central Terminal, the traveling fireman was waiting with open arms as the engine off #8 from Winsdor, Ont., which was to go through to Harmon, was cut out because of some mechanical trouble, and the 5408 was to be substituted. I told the traveling fireman that the engine was not steaming and the water pump would not supply the boiler but that didn't bother him at all. Well, I figured he knew what he was doing, who was a greenhorn like me to tell him his business. I guess they did all right with the engine though as I never heard any more about it. I wasn't worried about that though as much as I was about the excessive speed that was traveled from Suspension to Buffalo. If they read that tape when it was pulled at Huron, the Hogger and I would have both been in the sat

chel. Never heard anything about that either, so it went unnoticed. Another trip like that one though and I would have been looking for another way to make a living.

The experience related about the 5408 is really the only harrowing one I had. One I had though that was a little odd happened after I returned home from the service. I got called one night for #58 "The Cleveland Limited". It was a cold, bitter night in February, the temperature hovering around the 10 degree below mark. When the train pulled in to Central Terminal off the lines west, the 5432 was on the business end. When I climbed into the cab, the fireman I relieved told me how he was blowing the stoker jets and other conditions about the engine. He then promptly departed the cab leaving me to figure the rest of it out myself. He never said anything about the stoker being an off model, compared to the standard we were used to. There before my eyes was a Hanna stoker. Now this type stoker was foreign to us as there were only two engines in main line service equipped thusly. One, the 5432 and the other was an L-2, the 2706. I had fired the 2706 the first trip I made when I came back to work from the service but it was a long time in between that time and when I caught #58. My luck held out though and I tuned in Syracuse upon leaving Buffalo and the fire turned out beautifully. These Hanna stokers were a beautiful piece of mechanical works. They were only on these two engines as an experiment. I understand the reason the Central did not go for the Hanna jobs was because of the many working parts as compared to the Standard stokers. The P. & L. E. "Pacifics" were equipped with the Hannas and I believe they were the only other ones that had them on. But the stokers made by Standard, especially the H-T type, were just about the best you could get for firing an engine. All the fellows around the Syracuse Division and also the "Mohawkers" would have no other if it were up to them.

Another thing that made the 5400's the "Queens" of the fleet were the changes made in the front end and the removal of the Elesco water pumps for the more worthy Wothington pumps. The front ends were changed to what is called a Selkirk front end. This front end created a better draft in the firebox enabling the fire to burn better and increased the steaming qualities of the engines. I believe the reason I had so much trouble with the 5408 stemmed from this fact. All the Hudsons I fired that were so equipped, and also the 30 & 3100's along with the Niagaras, would burn cobblestones and stay hot over the road. The Selkirk front ends also sharpend the exhaust to a certain extent, also made them much prettier to listen to when they had a string of those old standard heavy weight

Pullmans behind them.

From Joseph N. Merchant, Framingham, Mass.
"Yes, I fired the 600's from 1939 to 1942. I fired for Fred Bennett on Train 26, The 20th Century (New England State after 1938) for over a year out of Boston to Springfield and returned on Train 40 to Boston. We never had a failure! I was set up in January 1942 and stayed on the spare board until after the war. I had the pleasure of running the 600's many trips while on the spare board.

I remember one night Train 26 came into Springfield station over 12 hours late. The temperature was near zero. There was a bad snow storm out through New York State with high drifts and cold weather which delayed the train. When train 26 came into Springfield station it was about 2 a.m. The traveling engineer helped us clean the fire and we finally left town. Going up Springfield hill, we discovered the water pump was not putting water in the boiler; the supply line was frozen. I immediately put on my injector, and every so often I would brake the injector and blow steam back through the supply hose to keep it thawed out. It was so cold the ceiling of the cab was white with frost. We finally made it without losing any time from Springfield to Boston.

I really enjoyed running this class of engine. It was so nice and easy to operate and could get a train over the road beautifully. When the Changeover was made from the 600's to the big Diesels, we seemed to lose interest in railroading but we had to keep up with progress.

My railroad service was from 1912 to 1957.

Edward C. Krupp, Briarcliff Manor, N.Y.
"I can say that I had the good fortune of being one of the men who handled this class of engine, and can say that it was not only a classic beauty in appearance, but also scored 100% in the performance department.

In reply to your question as to whether I liked or disliked this engine, I can say it did everything asked of it and was a pleasure to operate. It certainly steamed well and as for speed, it was always there and if necessary, it had a reserve power you could call upon to make-up lost time.

One thing I must say is that the NYC had the finest power and never lacked for anything needed to successfully complete a run.

Our railroad was the best that could be had — four mainline tracks from Grand Central Terminal to Albany, the end of our Division.

This mainline was always maintained in the very finest condition. The only place that was not four tracks was through the Hudson Highlands, where on account of the high rocks, space did not permit four tracks — this was a distance of six miles, from Peekskill to Garrison.

The one thing that happened to me was coming east on Train No. 8 — the "Wolverine" — east of Peekskill, the tire of the middle driver came off, but fortunately, the engine was not derailed. I must say that my days as an engineer were highly successful for which I thank the Good Lord.

Arnold H. Ainsworth, R.F.D., Ravena, N.Y.
To start off with I'm an engineer on River Div. of N.Y.C. commonly referred to as the West Shore we run from Weehawken to Selkirk. All freight as well as passenger service was discontinued back in 1959 I believe.

I ran and fired many of the 5200 & 5300 as well as B&A 600 to 619. I fired train 9 & 12 Weehawken N.J. to Albany, N.Y. for a few years and had one of the before mentioned engines. Train #9 usual was a heavy job consisting of twelve to fifteen cars. Mostly baggage cars but always a mail car and two coaches. #9 made all the local stops from Newburgh, N.Y. to Albany and those engines could really play with that job.

They were a nice engine I think the finest I ever was on. They sure could run as they used to wheel the passenger jobs 80 MPH on the Hudson and Mohawk Div. and even faster around Chicago and the south west. But the speed limit was 55 MPH on River Div.

Sometimes we would get one where speed recorder didn't work then we let them out a little. They made all kinds of steam on most any kind of coal. The harder you hit them the better they liked it or they would hang right up going light.

They had lots of power and could do a nice job on a freight train. And used as a helper double heading with a freight hog you couldn't beat them.

During World War Two we handled a lot of big troop trains heavy ones twenty cars or more. They came from the west and went to Camp Shanks at Orangeburgh, N.Y. which was an embarkment point. And much of the time we pulled these trains with the J engines or 5200 to 5300 and sometimes B&A 600 to 619.

When we had commuter service on River Div. we had a heavy fast job from Newburgh to Weehawken in the morning. Train #42 eight car local with a combo ahead as they unloaded mail. They always tried to keep a good engine on that job as it was needed towards the last of the steam era they took a B&A Hudson and put a small tank on her so they could get her on the turntable at Newburgh.

When she was on that job I caught the job off the Weehawken extra list and she sure could hit the ball on that job.

I caught that job lots of times and it seems to

me she was on there until the 8329 replaced her. An Alco jeep brand new.

I can truthfully say that I do not believe a better engine was ever built that could out run them or outpull them for their size. A nice comfortable cab handled nice, everything handy. All latest equipment at that time.

Harry J. Bengel, Dumont, N.Y.

During World War 2, I made a trip with a 5200 and 17 cars of war prisoners from Weehawken, N.J. to Selkirk, New York on the River Division of the New York Central 138 miles. The Assistant Supt, Train Master and Army Officers were trying to get train moving, because we were due in Selkirk at 8 a.m. Although we left over 1 hour late due to rain storm. I made up my mind to get there on time if possible. In spite of slow orders and a 50 mile speed limit, I let her out to about 70 to 75 miles per hour.

This may not seem very fast but our division with bridges and curves seems very fast. We arrived at Selkirk at 8:05 a.m. Met train Master the following day he asked me how I made out. I told him O.K. then he told me that he was going to tell me to step on it, but he didn't because he knew I would. A few days later I was on fast freight WB/5, crossing Catskill Bridge I exceeded the 30 mile speed by 6 miles, was called to see Ass't Supt., because an excess of 5 miles was the maximum allowable speed over the bridge. During the discussion that followed I asked him why I was not called up for exceeding speed limit with P.O.W. train as I exceeded every slow order on division, end of discussion. As I think about it we had quite a few of these discussions account of speed. They called me Hot Rod.

On another occasion I was running an express and mail train from Weehawken to Albany 154 miles and return with train 8. I let fireman run train part of the way up, time being slow I did not notice he was using straight air until I smelled something hot I stopped the train found right main tire hot, after arriving at Albany station left train and took engine to roundhouse at Rensselear, as I arrived at the pit, tire dropped off, I had a lot of explaining to do.

With a special of 20 cars, we hit a car with trailer while traveling 50 miles per hour, we cut the trailer off which was full of garbage. It covered the locomotive from the front end into cab, with beer cans, bed springs and other assorted junk. The traveling fireman was hit on head received bad cut. The State Police arrived and we went back looking for car it never returned, reason it had old plates on.

My first road trip just before the 16 hour went in effect. I was 36 hours going to Ravena, N.Y. with freight train with Engr. Hotaling, and return with Engr. Artman 37 hours. I guess I cleaned fires and ash pans about 10 times each way, we did not miss a side track or coal Pocket or Water tank we were passed by No.9 passenger train twice on the way up. After arriving at Ravena our eating and sleeping quarters was out in the swamps, where we slept on cots and eat in the same car. Believe me the food was terrible.

I ran both J1 and J2. I did like the J1 best it was very fast, easy handling.

H. W. Luhman, Ft. Pierce, Fla.

During the early 1930's I was on the Harmon extra fireman's list.

Train 31 was a N.Y. to Albany local express. After leaving Hudson Station our next stop was Albany. Train consisted of 9 or 10 coaches — speed limit there on Track 2 and 1 was 80 MPH. About 3 miles west Stuyvesant, the Engine gave a terrific lurch and continuous pounding gave me the frightening feeling we were going to turn over on the left side. The engineer immediately dumped her or set the brakes in emergency position. At 80 MPH it took about ½ mile to bring the train to a stop. This was the longest half mile ride I ever had, although lasting only about 1½ minutes.

The main rod on the right side of engine snapped about 2 feet from cross-head shoe. The entire right side of the engine was stripped. Lap and lead lever — union link — main eccentric rod, etc. Some part of which hit the blow-off cock on right side of the firebox thus allowing water to blow off. I really had to work fast to prevent burning the Crown Sheet the fire had to be dumped immediately. After shaking both front and rear (right) grates, I realized the temperature outside was about 10° below zero, so I saved the fire on the left rear grate so we could have some heat in the cab with the fire door open. This amount of fire would not damage Crown or Side Sheets with the door open.

It was quite an experience coming to a stop with the part of the main rod attached to driving wheel digging into the ties and road bed and water and steam blowing from right side of firebox — plus the water dropping in both water glass gauges.

After about 2 hours, relief engine arrived from Rensselaer with 7 or 8 roundhouse mechanics. In the bitter cold of 10° below it took about 2 more hours to prepare engine to be towed.

It was a J-1 engine and I do not have a record to verify the number of it.

Train 29 (The Niagara) was single-tracked at Stuyvesant and stopped alongside of us about 30 minutes after the break-down and took our passengers to Albany.

I found out later that the main rod had snapped on account of tractional fracture due to wear.

I fired from 1920 to 1940 on the Hudson Div. and worked as Engineer, both Freight and Passenger from 1940 to Nov. 1963 on all J1-2 and J3 engines.

My favorite and sweetheart was the "5400". They took a little longer to accelerate on account of having a smaller diameter delivery pipe to the valves, but once you gained acceleration, no other engine in the J class could give you more speed or a better ride.

Si Herring, Bellefontaine, Ohio

"I remember when I worked 3rd trick in the "house" as a grease cup filler. Boy, I can see it now, around 3:20 A.M. every night right after lunch and when everyone who has any sense was in bed where they belonged. The hottest thing on the agenda every night was getting the Big J off 38 for 41. 38 due in around 2:30 A.M., up over #2 ash pit which was always held clear for a fire cleaning while the outside inspector went over 'er with a fine tooth comb. The foreman in the office huddled over the engine dispatcher's shoulder while the engineer reeled off the items he wanted fixed. The tension in the air until the hogger finished to see if there was anything drastic that would kill the engine right there. Then the foreman trotting out to 18 stall with the report while all the men hovered around in the dim light to see what jobs they had to do. You could hear the old big J's drivers thump on the turntable joints and the alemite man and I would have our stuff spotted raring to go the minute the wheels stopped turning. I had my big grease gun air hose all ready to hook on to the air pump connection the minute she stopped and another few seconds had the gun fitting on the main pin shooting the sticks of grease which looked like dynamite into the pins. The alemite man would be ready to go on the valve gear with his little puny outfit, which went, pft, pft while my gun cracked like a shot every time I pulled the trigger. The cellar packer put the blue flag on and was down under the engine inspecting the driving box cellars. The poor old machinist with his huge wrenches on his shoulder, the special appliance man with his little kit of tools, the boiler maker — "hot man" and his helper up in the cab inspecting the crown sheet. Then came the electrician the best job of all with his tools, a screw driver and pliers stuck in his bib overalls and little testing bar in hand to hold under the ATS receiver while the helper pulled the forestall lever in the cab waiting for the little "beep-beep". Everyone gives 'er the quick finishing touches, signs the work report while the cellar packer removes the blue flag and the foreman jerks the work report tin off the pilot grab iron, hollers to the hostler, "take 'er away, Bill" and we all stand clear while the jockey opens the cylinder cocks and eases the throttle out shooting steam all over the place. After she thumps to a stop the old merry-go-round motor whines as she lines up to the outbound ready track. Our work is done and we look at the watch, 3:40 A.M., just 20 minutes in the house. She heads for the coal dock where another gang takes over coaling, sanding and taking water while the hostler washes the deck down the helper fills the water jug and gets a chunk of ice if it is in the summer and the old girl is set over on #2 outbound to rest a few minutes until the outbound crew shows up for 41. I can hear the air pumps thumping now just like the old iron monster was alive and breathing, the dynamo purring like a kitten. Man, those were the days and we would sure be a lot better off if they were back, the steamers I mean.

Si Herring relates the words of an un-named engineer.

Here is somthing he says, "Moments you'd like to live forever", such as catching the firing job on the old Knickerbocker, #24, with a good steaming J-1, rollin' into depot at Terre Haute always a big passenger town. Everything going fine, with a good hogger to work with and as you roll in sittin' there hanging out the window by your toes with a turned up bill cap, cigar, and big goggles on. As you roll by the platform all the people looking up at you with envy and you wouldn't trade your job for the President's. Then jumpin' up off the seat and slidin down the hand rails or grab irons before she stops, drop off and catch the tender step and climb up on the tank to take water. All the kids standing there with eyes big as saucers wishing they could take your place. Boy, he says that was a good feeling. Then you get a highball and kick the spout around and climb over the coal space to finish a fast trip to Indpls. Them were the days he says.

Then another trip with old "Low water" Chambers, the hogger who always ran every water plug he could and kept you scared to death all the way wondering if you could make it to the next water plug with the eerie sound of the low water alarm half way over the road. Engines steamed better that way if the boiler wasn't full.

Next trip you get the 52 somethin or other, a noted bad steamer and fightin it all the way over the road, shaking grates and working your ass off, on the mail and express just ahead of #12, wondering if you'll keep ahead of him or at least make the next siding so you can go in the hole for 'im without delay'n him and then have to see the road foreman and explain why. Or worse yet the road foreman might be waiting at the station platform with his big hams waving and shoutin his lungs out. Them was the days, full of steam failures, plugged flues, front end plugged, arch plugged, throat sheet plugged, stoker broke down, clinkered fires, etc., bad coal or real estate as they called it. Gad, I can hear them now, making out a work report, engine won't steam, grates cocked, piston packing blowing, injector don't work, water pump won't work, wonder how they got water in one like that, poured it in with a bucket I guess.

Si Herring interviews fireman Bill Bowman.

"He was telling me about an engineer Walker Terrill, you would have to know him to appreciate this as he was one who made more fast runs and switched more cars at the YMCA with a crowd around him. Bill Bowman, this fireman, said he listened to that s - - t for about a half hour and then said, "Walker, you might got by with all that stuff on NYC but I've boomed around a bit and you sure wouldn't have done it on the old I. J. & S. I." Walker says what road is that. "That is the old Ireland, Jerusalem & Southern Indiana, didn't you ever hear of it? "We run passenger trains so long and the cars so big the conductor rode a motorcycle thru the train and punched the tickets with a six shooter." Old Walker just picked up his grip and went to bed without saying another word.

I asked him if he had any stories of J-1's. He said he did fire a few on passenger and one time out of here on old 407 he had the 5332, a good steamer but rough rider, with the "ever alert" Eagle Eye, Red Hartman (another character confined to yards now from hitting a caboose last Feb. at Muncie and breaking the flagman's arm). They took off out of Bellefontaine, engine steaming good and everything going fine. A few miles out of town the engine was steadily picking up speed and running square as a die. As they progressed Bill thought she was riding a little rough and noticed the telephone poles going by like a picket fence. He looked at the side rods and instead of going up and down they were just flutterin in the middle. He hollered at Red and said something about the speed and old Red had that glazed look in his eye looking about the countryside and wondering if his uranium stock, which he bought from another fireman who also was a stock promoter, was going up or down. Finally Red come out of the fog and looked at the speed recorder. About this time Bill didn't know whether to stick with the engine or jump off. Old Red says, my, my how these engines do creep up before you know it, 93 miles an hour. He cushioned the throttle and brought her down to 75 which was the limit at that time. Then to top it off he zips right through Sidney, a regular stop. The conductor set the air on him and he had to back up. At the time Red was just an extra man on passenger and he says, "Hell, the last time I was on here Sidney was a flag stop, I looked and didn't see no flag out or passengers on the platform although there was about 4 trucks of mail but thought that was for loading to the post office." By the way it was Bill's first trip after being furloughed and Red lost his timetable at the Y before going out, what a bunch of cards.

Incidentally Red was an the lead engine of 304 one night coming this way, he had a J-1 and Wildcat McCoy was on the second engine with an L-4. Again coming out of Sidney eastbound after winding 'em Wildcats engine stripped itself and the Right Main driver went rolling out in a cornfield. I never thought you could lose a drive wheel, didn't think it could get out with the side rods and main rod holding but it did. Poor old Red and Wildcat both got 10 days over that for not noticing the driving box which should have gotten a fine cherry red before it let go. The fireman with Wildcat told me he thought the world came to an end with all the clatter and noise and dust flying. Lucky nothing derailed.

From Alvin Staufer, Medina, Ohio

After reading everyone else's experiences, I must share mine. Having been reared in the Cleveland area I have observed Hudsons scads of times and in every conceivable circumstance but my fondest memory was a certain trip as a passenger.

It was early in Dec. 1943, on a long weekend leave from Navy Diesel School at Navy Pier in Chicago. There was the opening stampede of thousands of sailors from the pier to the various railroad stations. Trolleys were the vehicle and how they held so many, or why we weren't killed by hanging on by our fingernails is one of those mysteries of survival we won't explore right now, but God it was cold!

We invade LaSalle St. station, get tickets and swarm in a huge circle around the gate. We can glimpse the waiting trains, row upon row of coaches with steam drifting up between the cars and the distant engines ahead.

The conductor, or whoever it is that works the gates, hollers ALL ABOARD, then unlatches the grill and leaps back as the crush of humanity pours through. Nobody walks, everybody is running full speed, even civilians. The name of the game is "get a seat" and us smart money boys head as far forward as we can get.

Exactly 36 seconds after the gate is open the train is full, every seat, every aisle; there is barely room for the conductors to squeeze through. You sit there panting and why not, you have just broken the world's record for the 3/8 mile. This car is about 2/3 service men with a generous helping of fast (running that is) girls.

Last ALL ABOARD is called and we move out. We are in the second car behind the engine so we hear and feel it all. We move through the yard and head south by buildings and stock yards. The sheer size of Chicago always amazed me. It seems like you'd get home before you ever got out of that place. Remember stopping at Englewood but don't know where they ever put those people.

Finally, you begin to move into open country. You can hear the "snap" of the accelerating exhaust. Now you are doing about 80 MPH. It's about 4:30 and approaching twilight. Scenery is flashing by. And then you notice it, that pulsating high speed throb that was unique with steam and steam alone. God we were flying. There was no snow on the ground, it was getting darker, lights begin to flash by.

Your attention is drawn inside to the crush of noisy happy people. Soon the music starts. Don't know if it was, the WAR, the TIMES or what, but group singing just seemed to happen back then. Just like on a hay-ride or something. First its a small cell, then it just spreads through the whole car. Songs were real scorchers like — "Over There", "Seeing Nellie Home", "Me and My Gal" — "Shine on Harvest Moon" and a whole raft of special service songs.

The racket was just beautiful. Over 100 people in the middle of "It's a Long Way to Tipperary" — off key — the whole shot. Out there in front is that damned Hudson, every so often joining in with its mornful screams. Boy, talk about chills. That mass of pulsating steel, thinks it's alive. Now I know that it was.

Looking back and reliving it through these words it really appears corny as hell, but that was a different world, a different us, a different America. I'll say this. If things like that could be purchased, I'd lay out one thousand dollars RIGHT NOW to live that trip again.

Fourteen years ago, I wrote a brief story and created this illustration. We spare you the entire prose that went briefly like this.
    On a Fall evening in October, 1960, a guy pulls his car over along side the New York Central mainline to watch the Twentieth Century Limited come by. Instead of diesels and two tone gray this specter from the past comes roaring along. He is obviously moved by the entire scene particularly when he remembers the marker lights were shining green.
    Will another apparition from 1927 appear? Will he wait to watch for it?

For that split second their eyes met!

WHAT FOLLOW

ED

Robert A. Whitbeck

Forte of all Hudsons was power at speed. The tractive assist of the booster was an absolute necessity when starting. This is an accepted fact, penalty if you will, when perpetually squeezing the maximum from a relatively small locomotive.

Let's analyze the booster and see what is involved. First, there is the expense and maintenance of a very complex piece of machinery. You must educate your men to use it properly and that's never a 100% proposition. Steam and exhaust lines total about 100 feet and that's a lotta line. It isn't worth a hoot without sand and there just have to be easier places to put sand than a 51" wheel underneath the firebox.

Wouldn't it be simpler to just add a driving axle and drop the booster? We are not implying that the New York Central adopted the four coupled locomotive just because of the booster, but we are saying that there was a change of philosophy and thinking towards larger locomotives — period!

On January 1, 1932, Patrick E. Crowley turned over the reins of the New York Central to Frederick E. Williamson. Raymond D. Starbuck became system's Executive Vice President at this time.

Soon after the last J3's were built, Starbuck summoned Kiefer to his Park Avenue suite for an overall evaluation of motive power. Pending need was freight, but problems were developing at peak passenger periods. It was at this meeting that the

L4 3102 just off the track pans westbound into a late afternoon sun at Rome, New York.

Al Staufer collection

Above: Rebuilt Mohawk 2995 at Selkirk, New York. June, 1946.
Right: Since 2998 had roller bearings on all wheels, (except trailing truck) it was selected for display at the World's Fair in New York, June, 1940.

Edward L. May

dual purpose (freight and passenger) concept was born. Final decision was to convert two of the latest built freight 4-8-2 Mohawks for passenger service. Mohawks were often pressed into service, but were limited to 60 m.p.h., partly for their own preservation. Every steam locomotive's rods and counterweights were designed for its specific usage and speed range.

The chosen Mohawks (L2d's 2995 & 2998, Alco 1930) were converted in the following manner:
  Boiler pressure raised from 225 lbs. to 250 lbs.;
  New lightweight reciprocating parts;
  Dynamic counterbalancing of all drivers;
  Roller bearings on all wheels engines and tenders except drivers on 2995 and trailer trucks of either engine;
  Cast steel pilot with drop coupler;
  Alterations raised engine weights from about 370,150 to 385,000 lbs., and total tractive force from 73,000 lbs. to 73,850 lbs. including booster;
  Drivers remained 69";
  Same tenders, 15,000 gals., 28 tons.

If any lingering hopes for more Hudsons were prevalent, they were dispelled when the two Mohawks were tested. They were utterly fantastic. 3,800 cylinder horsepower was developed at 45 m.p.h., and track damage was no more than any Hudson at speeds up to 87 m.p.h. All this on small 69" drivers.

2995 and 2998 became the protype for 65 additional 4-8-2's to be built between 1940-42. Major differences were spacing to allow 72" drivers if ever wanted; bigger combustion chamber; tender capacity increased to 15,500 gals., 43 tons.

They were:
L3a, 3000-3034 (Alco) dual purpose with roller bearings on all wheels, no booster engine;
L3b, 3035-3049 (Lima) freight, roller bearings on all wheels except drivers;
L3c, 3050-3064 (Alco) freight, roller bearings on all wheels except drivers.

The L3a's were clearly superior to the Hudsons particularly on rated horsepower up to 50 m.p.h. This made them better suited for heavier passenger trains. Above that speed the L3a Mohawks had all the power necessary for sustained high speeds.

This leads us to speculate what would have happened if the two L2d Mohawks had been converted in 1935 instead of 1939. Probably very little. Super flyers were needed for coming streamliners and there was no freight power shortage at that time. The

L3b Mohawk 3029 at Bellefontaine, Ohio.   William Swartz

J3's were already on the drawing boards and all concerned were dedicated to this super engine. The Hudson just had too much tradition and momentum going for it. It may have resulted in a reduction of the J3 order of 50 units. Oh, well, we're just as good at "Monday morning quarterbacking" as the next guy.

New York Central needed more locomotives in 1942 and there was absolutely no question as to what they would order. They wanted dual purpose 4-8-2's. The country was at war and Uncle Sam was now calling the shots. No development time was permitted; "existing designs must be used", so an order was placed with Lima Locomotive Works for 50 L4's. Why Lima? Because wartime allocation of locomotive production said so, that's why!

The L4's were virtual duplicates of the dual service L3a's with these exceptions:
Drivers were 72" instead of 69", front end was the flat "Selkirk" style and neither class had booster engines. They were a marvelous machine earmarked for freight but needs dictated otherwise.

"The 50 L4's made 4,874,678 miles in passenger service and 1,099,315 miles in freight service in 1944; the 65 L3's made 882,173 miles in passenger service, and 3,288,241 miles in freight service."* Remember though, that only 25 of the 65 L3's were dual service type.

The dual purpose L4's clearly outclassed the Hudsons in every way except super fast sustained high speed runs like the Century and "Empire State Express." Their versatility was the delight of the

* "Forty Years of Motive Power Progress on the New York Central", Alco 1945.

New York Central

2995 with specially operated train of stator frames, rotors and condensers rolling by Cleveland's lakefront bound for West Coast shipyards.

307

First L4 Mohawk 3100 and string of new red and gray Pacemaker box cars at Garrison, New York. April 16, 1946.

Ed Nowak - New York Central

operating department. Visualize one pulling into LaSalle St. Station on the head of a 20 car limited. It would proceed to the enginehouse for service, where the enginehouse foreman would then have the option of sending her east on a hot-shot priority freight or another long passenger train.

Early in 1944 the New York Central prevailed upon the War Production Board and received permission to build an experimental super dual purpose 4-8-4 locomotive. Why they didn't tell them to go out and buy 25 more L4's we don't know, but we're mighty glad they didn't.

Many American Railroads made the big switch to the 4-8-4 type in the mid 1930's, but the Water Level Route just had to do things in their own time. Their time had come. Engineering began in April, 1944 and first Niagara was completed in March, 1945. And what a magnificent machine it was, enormous in every dimension. Grate area was 101 sq. ft., drivers were 75" (later replaced with 79"). No. 6000 hit the scales at 471,000 lbs.

New York Central had finally developed the ultimate steam locomotive. You name it and the mighty Niagara could pull it, from a 100 car freight to an endless limited. The 6000's had POWER and that power came from the drivers! It would have been insulting to stick a clinky booster on these behemoths. It was needed about as much as a Christmas tree sticking out of the stack.

They were loved to a point of worship by the men who ran them. Riding quality equaled that of a Pullman and steam was absolutely inexhaustible

Back to the six thousands. The 27 Niagaras were the largest and the last steam passenger locomotives built for the New York Central. They had it all, almost. The "mighty ones" had one inherent flaw, they were born too late. By the time Central got around to it, the show was over.

They were our kind of locomotive. Build 'em big and work 'em easy.

Ed Nowak - New York Central   6023 leaving yard at Albany at beginning of test run.

A view of the huge erection shop in Beech Grove, Indiana. In the foreground is the stripped down boiler of Niagara 6013.

William Swartz

SNOW

H. S. Ludlow

Niagara westbound through Vermilion, Ohio. Train appears to be just starting up after being held up by a red block. Consist is 14 mail and express cars and rider combine for crew.

NIAGARA

Arnold Haas

Fearful! And we can feel the speed and power. Looking back from fireman's side as Niagara takes water at 80 mph over the pans near Tivoli, New York.

NEW YORK CENTRAL SYSTEM

NIAGARA

Niagara 6003 leaving Chicago's La Salle Street Station with Limited in 1946.
  The Niagara could easily keep on schedule with 20 car limiteds while Hudsons needed ideal conditions to do the same.

Jim Seacrest collection

OTHER HU

SONS

The Hudson class 4-6-4 locomotive did not exactly sweep the country by storm. In the entire United States less than 500 were built and a few of these were created in company shops from older locomotives. Deducting these, we have OVER half of all Hudsons built in America going to the New York Central Railroad.

When one begins discussing numbers of a specific wheel arrangement doing what job on a given railroad, relative traffic must be taken into consideration. For example: Milwaukee Road's fleet of 28 F6 & F7 Hudsons represented the second largest fleet of 4-6-4's in the U.S.A.; not very impressive when compared with Central's 275. But, what percent of each road's passenger miles did the 28 and 275 haul respectively? The ratio is probably quite close. What one tends to overlook in these comparisons is the enormous size of the New York Central and its very high percentage of passenger train miles.

The figures we always "throw about" to dramatize "size" is to compare the number of 4-8-2's owned by the Chesapeake & Ohio and N.Y.C. The C & O pioneered the type and had 10; Central had exactly 600.

Wabash Hudson running with the "City of St. Louis". Engine was rebuilt from a 2-8-2 Mikado type.

Illinois Central's only Hudson was rebuilt from 2-8-4 No. 7038 which was originally built by Lima in 1926. I.C. shops did the work in 1937 and engine is shown here at Markham, Ill. October, 1938.
Harold K. Vollrath

C&O had the heaviest Hudsons. L2 305 was built by Baldwin in 1942 and weighed 439,500 lbs. Drivers were 78" and grate area 90 sq. ft. Five Hudsons, also by Baldwin, built for the C&O in 1948 were the last to be built in America.
Harold K. Vollrath

Second largest fleet of Hudsons on the Continent was Canadian Pacific's 65 units, classes H1a-H1e. They were about the same size as Central's J's, with slightly smaller (75") drivers. Some were built or rebuilt without steam domes and partial streamlining, giving them a unique British (Continental) American appearance.

Largest and last Hudsons were the five built by Baldwin for the C & O in 1948. Drivers were 78" and engine weight was 443,000 lbs. (J1e's weighed 351,000 lbs.) They never did "chintz" on iron or size down there in Philadelphia.

Largest practical driver diameter for the 4-6-2 Pacific was 80" but the Hudson could and did in four instances have more. 84" drivers were used in part by the Santa Fe, B & O, Chicago & North Western, and Milwaukee Road. They were all massive magnificent machines.

Smallest fleet of Hudsons belonged to the Illinois Central who had just one. Rebuilt locomotive number was — "one".

Hudsons most similar in appearance to New York Central's were the five built for the DL & W (Lackawana). And well they should, as they were built by American Locomotive Co. at the same time the J3's were under construction.

The neatest looking rebuilds, in our opinion, were the 10 undertaken by the St. Louis & San Francisco (Frisco Lines).

Milwaukee Road's first 14 Hudsons class F6, had a rather gangley look, sort of jumbled and simply "not neat and trim". If American Locomotive Co. had a slavish devotion to the horizontal line, then the exact opposite could be said of the Baldwin Loco Works. They seemed to delight in exterior fixtures of disorganized array. Later Hudsons by Baldwin for this same road displayed a marked improvement in appearance.

TOTAL CONTINENT PRODUCTION
4-6-4 HUDSON TYPE

RAILROAD	ALCo (US)	ALCo (Canada)	LIMA	BALDWIN	COMPANY SHOPS	TOTAL
Santa Fe				16		16
Boston & Albany (NYC)			10			20
Baltimore & Ohio					4	4
Canadian National		5				5
Canadian Pacific		65				65
Chesapeake & Ohio				13	5	18
Chicago & Northwestern	9					9
Burlington				12		12
Milwaukee Road	6			22		28
Lackawanna	5					5
Illinois Central					1	1
Maine Central				2		2
Mexico	10					10
New York Central	255					255
Nickel Plate	4		4			8
New Haven				10		10
Frisco					10	10
Wabash					7	7
TOTALS	299	70	14	75	27	485

Only other railroad known to have operated 4-6-4 type was TH&B which bought two NYC second-hand.

SUMMARY

We will attempt to analyze why these magnificent machines (4-6-4 Hudson type) didn't sweep the entire land and haul most of the passenger trains the last three decades of steam in America. Foremost, and as we have stated many times, they were a unique machine particularly adapted to the profile of the New York Central, they were long haul, high speed, level run flyers. This would easily explain why roads like say, the Pennsy and B & O couldn't utilize the type to its best advantage, but there are many others that could — but didn't. Why Not?

Remember, we are only speculating here. Anyway, we feel that timing of development was a major and limiting influence. It was born just prior to the depression. We're certain that many other railroad motive power executives looked upon the princely Water Level performance with a twinge of awe and envy.

Who wouldn't want them?

Surely, serious discussion and preliminary studies were undertaken. So what happened? The depression happened. During four to five years (1931-1935) new locomotive orders in America practically dried up; 1931 - 176 (most of these were Central J's). 1932 - 12, 1933 - 42, 1934 - 183 and 1935 - 87

In that interim slumber there emerged the dominance of a new dual purpose super locomotive, the 4-8-4. Sort of like waking up in the morning to a whole new ball game. That's the machine the boys wanted to put their money in; that and dual service super 4-8-2's. There's no denying their superiority to the Hudson in almost every way. Again we quote our previous statement — "The New York Central was dedicated to the type, it was destined to succeed itself", Thus we had the 50 super J3 Hudsons. Other roads had no such obligations to tradition. Some Hudsons were purchased, true, but due partly to the continuing economic squeeze, many roads simply rolled older engines (mostly Pacifics) into their major shops and created their own Hudsons. The Central itself actually "dropped" the type and turned completely to the four coupled drive.

Not counting the Central, only 103 Hudsons were built new for American railroads, certainly not an impressive figure. But things develop in their time and work out as they do.

They were destined to be built, if for no other reason than the logical expansion of the 4-6-2 Pacific. But had it not been for the large fleet of the second railroom in the land, the type would have been merely a small link joining the Pacifics of the 20's to the dual power of the 30's and 40's.

But it did happen, so the New York Central Hudson became the most famous class of steam locomotive in the world.

Nickel Plate Hudson, class L1a, Alco (Dunkirk) 1927, is one of eight. 74" drivers, 318,400 lbs., and grate area 66.7 sq. ft.

Harold K. Vollrath

Harold K. Vollrath   Maine Central, one of two, (701-702) built by Baldwin in 1930, 73" drivers, 315,590 lbs. and grate area 62.6 sq. ft. These were the smallest Hudsons and 702 was later sold to Portland Terminal.

One of B&O's four Hudsons, named the "Lord Baltimore", on the "Royal Blue" west of Pennington, N.J., April 1937. All four were built or rebuilt in company shops.

Harold K. Vollrath

New Haven's ten Hudsons (I5 Nos. 1400-1409) were built by Baldwin in 1937 and weighed 365,300 lbs. Drivers were 80″ and grate area 77.1 sq. ft.

Rail Photo Service

Milwaukee Road's F6 class, Baldwin 1930-31, is a far cry from the sleek J1 race horses found on the princely New York Central. Drivers were 80″, weight 375,850 lbs. and grate area 80 sq. ft.

Bob Lorenz

F7, No. 101, Alco 1938, 84″ drivers, 415,000 lbs. engine weight, 96.5 sq. ft. grate area and steam pressure 300 lbs.
   Massive beautiful machines designed by Otto Kuhler, superior to NYC's J3's in performance and maybe even looks. These were BIG enough to do the job while the Central's J3 were relatively small and pressed to the limits of their capacity.

Harold K. Vollrath

317

Harold K. Vollrath — Santa Fe's "Blue Goose", Chillicothe, Ill. Feb. 1948. Built by Baldwin in 1937 with 84" drivers, 98.5 sq. ft. grate area and engine weight 420,400 lbs. Obviously big and obviously blue.

Bob Yanosey collection — Wabash, 700-706, rebuilt at company shops from three-cylinder 2-8-2 Mikados — of all things. Engine weight 374,000 lbs., drivers 80" and grate area 70.9 sq. ft.

Most New York Central looking of all the other Hudsons were these five (1151-1155) built for the D.L.&W. (Lackawanna) by Alco in 1937. Drivers were 80", grate area 81.5 sq. ft., and engine weight 377,000 lbs.

Canadian Pacific Hudson were built by Montreal Loco Works (Alco) from 1929 to 1940 and were numbered 2800 to 2864. Drivers were 75", grate area 80.8 sq. ft., and engine weight 366,000 lbs. The last few built had boosters.

Similar to the Milwaukee Road's (pg. 317 bottom) were these nine (4001-4009) built for the C.&N.W. by Alco 1938. Drivers 84", grate area 90.7 sq. ft. and engine weight 412,000 lbs.

Delightfully complex! 4000-4004 were originally built by Baldwin in 1930 and rebuilt by Burlington Shops in 1937-38. Drivers were 78", grate area 87.9 sq. ft. and engine weight was 388,700 lbs. Square gadget between steam and sand dome is automatic train control.

Bob Lorenz

Ten engines (1060-1069) were rebuilt into Hudsons at the St. Louis-San Francisco company shops at Springfield, Mo. from 4-6-2 Pacifics that were originally built by Baldwin in 1917. 74" drivers, 82.5 sq. ft. grate and weight of 360,960 lbs. WE LIKE THESE.

Yanosey collection

319

TOYS AND MOI

Roger A. Rasor

In good ol' free enterprise America, sales count. Since the inception of the toy train industry it was apparent that the name NEW YORK CENTRAL lithographed on the tender or engine, meant just that — sales.

New York City based Lionel and Marx were quite naturally exposed to the glamour of "The Road of the Century". Ives of Bridgeport, Connecticut liked New Haven; but still, their favorite prototype was New York Central's "S" class electrics. Even American Flyer (way out in Chicago) accepted the magic of that name — New York Central.

It was never a question of which road was the most popular — actually, after the Hudson appeared, it became somewhat of a challenge to find a toy train that was not lettered or modeled after the NEW YORK CENTRAL RAILROAD.

Because of its simplicity and ease of manufacture, the "Commodore Vanderbilt" model was a great favorite, particularly with the lower priced train sets. The more numerous Dreyfuss styled Hudsons held less appeal in the toy line, but persisted nonetheless.

Highmark for all Hudson inspired toys was Lionel's 1937 J1e Hudson 5344. This was quite a departure for Joshua Lionel Cowen (the company's founder) for his firm had, for the past 33 years,

Scale "O" gauge Hudsons double head on author's "Twilight Limited". Lead engine is Max Gray B&A J2 Hudson and other is Scale-Craft J1. Sky was painted by Craig Staufer.

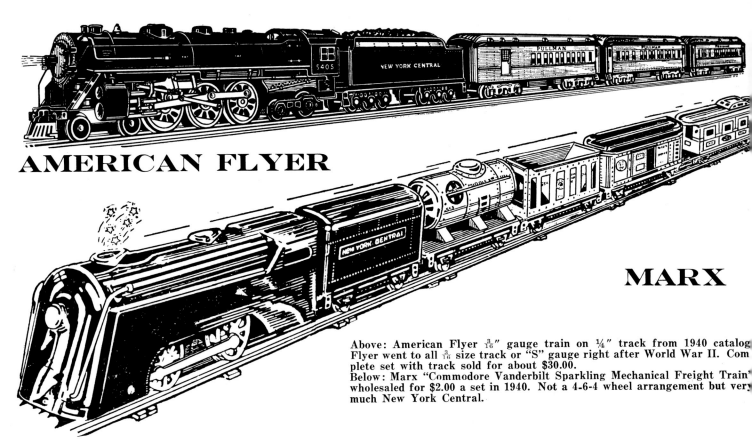

AMERICAN FLYER

MARX

Above: American Flyer $\frac{3}{16}$" gauge train on ¼" track from 1940 catalog. Flyer went to all $\frac{3}{16}$ size track or "S" gauge right after World War II. Complete set with track sold for about $30.00.
Below: Marx "Commodore Vanderbilt Sparkling Mechanical Freight Train" wholesaled for $2.00 a set in 1940. Not a 4-6-4 wheel arrangement but very much New York Central.

produced and promoted trains with a distinct "toy" flavor. Lionel's 5344 (700 E model number) was a ¼" masterpiece. It came mounted on a wooden plaque and sold for $75.00, no small amount in 1937. It was three rail with middle pick-up shoes, as were all toy trains of the period, and was designed to operate on wide radius 072 track.

It was also offered in a lesser detailed version (model 763) and was even built to 00" scale (a size between ⅛" and $\frac{3}{16}$" to the foot). The 700E was built from 1937 to 1942, when War contracts forced Lionel to suspend all toy manufacture. The scale version Hudson was never put back into production; this in spite of thousands of pleas from toy and scale modelers across the land.

Any model that is mass produced just has to be a compromise as it would be literally impossible to capture every detail. And herein lies the genius of Lionel's 700E Hudson. Proportions and dimensions were perfect; the only compromise being wheel flange size to run on toy tracks. Lionel design engineers included all parts necessary to capture the "feel" of the real thing, even to front drop coupler (which worked) and swinging smokebox front. Basic material of construction was the same as most toy trains of the period — cast Zamak, a zinc alloy. The earlier production models were prone to breakage due to impurities in the castings but Irvington (Lionel's New Jersey factory) soon corrected its techniques, resulting in more stable models.

In spite of its high price the model was immensely popular, selling by the thousands. After World War II, the semi-scale Hudson was produced on two different occasions but never again the fabulous 700E 5344.

The fame of Central's Hudsons was world-wide so it is no surprise that other countries used it as a basic model — particularly Germany. It's a known fact that American railroads are much more popular in Europe than theirs are here.

In 1929 the A. C. Gilbert Co. of New Haven produced an Erector Set that has to be one of the most spectacular toys ever built. It was offered in two sets, one for engine and one for tender. They were the conventional Erector Sets with the usual array of nuts, bolts and miscellaneous parts but the similarity ended there because they would only build one thing — a Hudson engine or Hudson tender. When assembled, the sets created a well proportioned New York Central Hudson of immense size. Length over couplers was 48" and height 8". The late 20's and early 30's were the era of the "big toys" in America and Gilbert's Hudson was one of the finest and biggest.

In scale model railroading, as in toys, New York Central's Hudson ranks as the most popular models selected for production.

Why this universal popularity? As we stated in the "Foreword", they were THE locomotive for THE road at the height of rail passenger travel in America. And maybe, just maybe, they were the most beautiful.

Centerfold from American Flyers 1957 catalog. Hudson is evident but "New York Central System" is small oval on tender. Die cast engine and tender purchased separately cost $44.00.

A. C. Gilbert

Strom-Becker ¼" wooden Hudson made about 1948. The company manufactured an entire series of various wooden trains in ¼" and ⅛" size.

Lionel

Lionel's 773 semi-scale Hudson re-introduced in 1964. No comment on the Pennsylvania tender.

LIONEL

323

AMERICAN FLYER

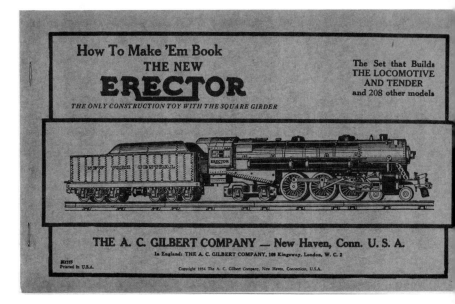

Instruction catalog for the gigantic E-RECTOR Hudson Locomotive and Tender which measured 48" x 7½" when completed. Set was offered from about 1929 to 1935.

Above: Erector Hudson and Lionels "OO" gauge Hudson which was about $\frac{5}{32}$" size. Right: We have Hudsons in three sizes. N gauge, O gauge and Erector which was about ½" gauge.

Roger A. Rasor

New York Central

New York Central draftsman, Reginald H. Claudius, hand crafted, these Central models in ½″ scale. Work was accomplished in his home basement with a minimum of power tools and all trains were designed to run.
Above. Claudius standing by his craft.
Below: His "Twentieth Century Limited" on display in Grand Central with engine 5200, "as built". We wonder where they are today.

No. 5200

New York Central

LIONEL 700E

Only instance we know of where a toy train manufacturer produced a catalog for a single engine. Lionel did in 1937 for its fabulous 700E NYC Hudson.

Lionel

Roger A. Rasor

We know that the Railroad selected 5344 because it was the last J1e built and had all roller bearings. Perhaps the Central recommended this to Lionel.

Center spread of Lionel's 700E catalog. Lionel's 1938 catalog contains a picture of System president Williamson posing with a model of 5344 beneath the portrait of Commodore Vanderbilt.

Lionel

Roger A. Rasor

Roger A. Rasor

It's obvious that if a scale "O" gauger owns matching builder's plate and number for a specific Hudson that he will letter one of his own in kind.

View on the author's scale "O" railroad has, left: Max Gray, Mohawk, middle: Max Gray streamlined Hudson with Twentieth Century Limited and right, 1902 Century. On upper level four track mainline are B&O and Pennsy trains.

Vance Roth

Nice shot of Central's first train, the DeWitt Clinton and a J3 super Hudson. DeWitt Clinton was built by Bill Lenoir and J3 was brass import from Japan by U. S. Hobbies.

U.S. HOBBIES J3

One advantage of toys is we can make comparisons between non-existant items. This is how big the 999 is when backed by a Super Hudson. 999 is built by Bill Lenoir and J3 is a U. S. Hobbies import; both from author's collection.

The largest model railroad and assemblage of scale "O" gauge that we know of is Mack Lowry's "Railways of America." On route 8, about five miles north of Akron, Ohio, it has literally hundreds of engines and hundreds of cars in a room about 50 x 170′ And, of course, in scale "O" — all things run.

Roger A. Rasor

Vance Roth

The perennial favorite, even of scale "O" gaugers, Lionel's 700E, No. 5344. Model here is insulated for scale 2-rail operation.

17/64 scale Mi-Loco NYC J1b Hudson. 17/64" is slightly larger than "O" scale (16/64) and came into being because scale "O" is slightly small for its track width of 1¼".

Scale "O" Hudson manufactured by Scale-Craft about 1940. This particular kit was assembled, detailed and painted by former "O" scale manufacturer Fred Icken. One of my favorites.

Scale "O" J3 Hudson imported by U. S. Hobbies. Model is of J3 "as built" with straight running board, regular tender, and reverse gear inside frame.

Scale "O" imported by Max Gray, predecessor of U. S. Hobbies, is J3 with Pt 2 tender.

Scale "O" line up of NYC power. Left to right: 999 and Lake Shore Ten Wheeler by Bill Lenoir, K3 Pacific by Herlberg, J1e Hudson by Lionel, L4 Mohawk by Max Gray, S1 Niagara by U. S. Hobbies and E7 EMD passenger diesels by Bill Lenoir.

Two views of same set up at "Railways of America" (see page 329) show "Century" and "Broadway" with respective power on each. This is all "O" Scale.

ART AND PLANS

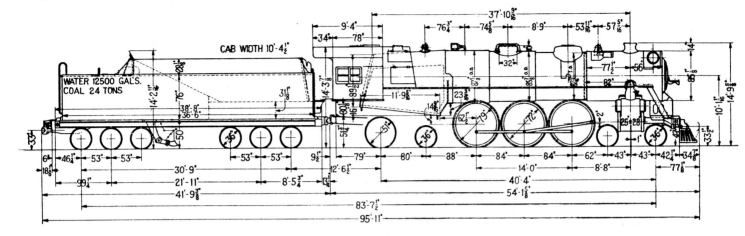

J1a 5200, other specifications same as below.

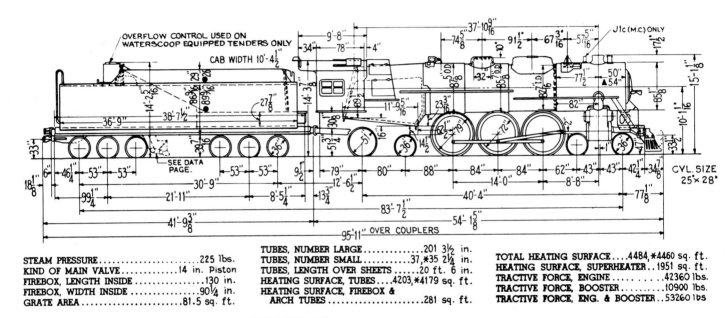

STEAM PRESSURE ..... 225 lbs.	TUBES, NUMBER LARGE ..... 201 3½ in.	TOTAL HEATING SURFACE ..... 4484, *4460 sq. ft.
KIND OF MAIN VALVE ..... 14 in. Piston	TUBES, NUMBER SMALL ..... 37, *35 2¼ in.	HEATING SURFACE, SUPERHEATER ..... 1951 sq. ft.
FIREBOX, LENGTH INSIDE ..... 130 in.	TUBES, LENGTH OVER SHEETS ..... 20 ft. 6 in.	TRACTIVE FORCE, ENGINE ..... 42360 lbs.
FIREBOX, WIDTH INSIDE ..... 90¼ in.	HEATING SURFACE, TUBES ..... 4203, *4179 sq. ft.	TRACTIVE FORCE, BOOSTER ..... 10900 lbs.
GRATE AREA ..... 81.5 sq. ft.	HEATING SURFACE, FIREBOX & ARCH TUBES ..... 281 sq. ft.	TRACTIVE FORCE, ENG. & BOOSTER ..... 53260 lbs

J1c, J1d, J1e SPECIFICATIONS.

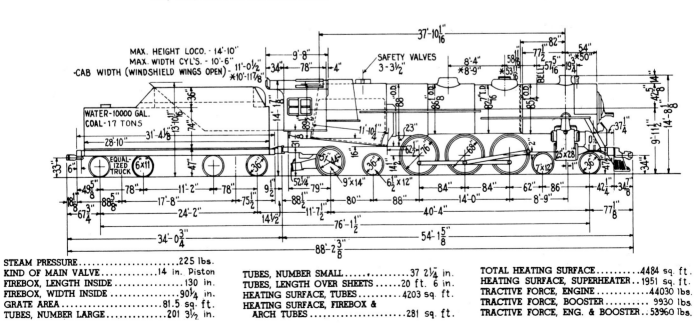

STEAM PRESSURE ..... 225 lbs.	TUBES, NUMBER SMALL ..... 37 2¼ in.	TOTAL HEATING SURFACE ..... 4484 sq. ft.
KIND OF MAIN VALVE ..... 14 in. Piston	TUBES, LENGTH OVER SHEETS ..... 20 ft. 6 in.	HEATING SURFACE, SUPERHEATER ..... 1951 sq. ft.
FIREBOX, LENGTH INSIDE ..... 130 in.	HEATING SURFACE, TUBES ..... 4203 sq. ft.	TRACTIVE FORCE, ENGINE ..... 44030 lbs.
FIREBOX, WIDTH INSIDE ..... 90¼ in.	HEATING SURFACE, FIREBOX & ARCH TUBES ..... 281 sq. ft.	TRACTIVE FORCE, BOOSTER ..... 9930 lbs.
GRATE AREA ..... 81.5 sq. ft.		TRACTIVE FORCE, ENG. & BOOSTER ..... 53960 lbs.
TUBES, NUMBER LARGE ..... 201 3½ in.		

BOSTON & ALBANY J2 SPECIFICATION.

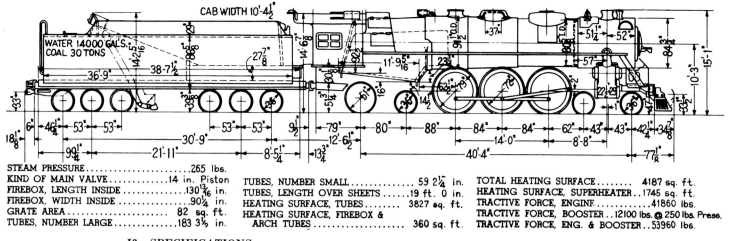

STEAM PRESSURE	265 lbs.	TUBES, NUMBER SMALL	59 2¼ in.	TOTAL HEATING SURFACE	4187 sq. ft.
KIND OF MAIN VALVE	14 in. Piston	TUBES, LENGTH OVER SHEETS	19 ft. 0 in.	HEATING SURFACE, SUPERHEATER	1745 sq. ft.
FIREBOX, LENGTH INSIDE	130 13/16 in.	HEATING SURFACE, TUBES	3827 sq. ft.	TRACTIVE FORCE, ENGINE	41860 lbs.
FIREBOX, WIDTH INSIDE	90¼ in.	HEATING SURFACE, FIREBOX & ARCH TUBES	360 sq. ft.	TRACTIVE FORCE, BOOSTER	12100 lbs. @ 250 lbs. Press.
GRATE AREA	82 sq. ft.			TRACTIVE FORCE, ENG. & BOOSTER	53960 lbs.
TUBES, NUMBER LARGE	183 3½ in.				

J3a SPECIFICATIONS.

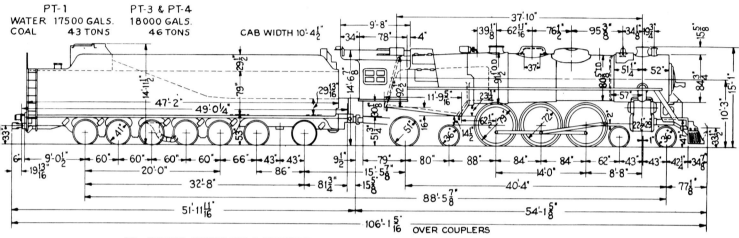

J3a SPECS. WITH PT 1 TENDER.

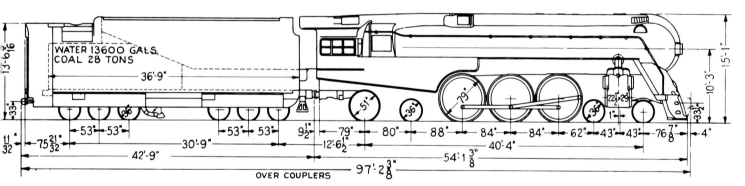

J3a STREAMLINED SPECIFICATION.

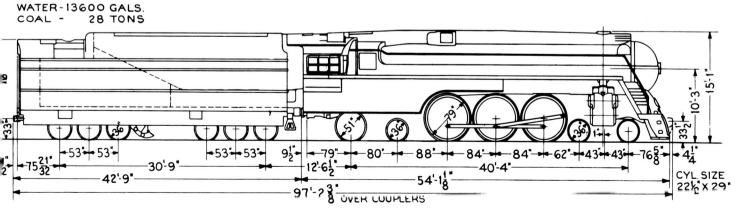

J3a's 5426 and 5429 "EMPIRE" SPECIFICATIONS.

334

NEW YORK CENTRAL J1 CLASS 4-6-4 HUDSON TYPE LOCOMOTIVE.

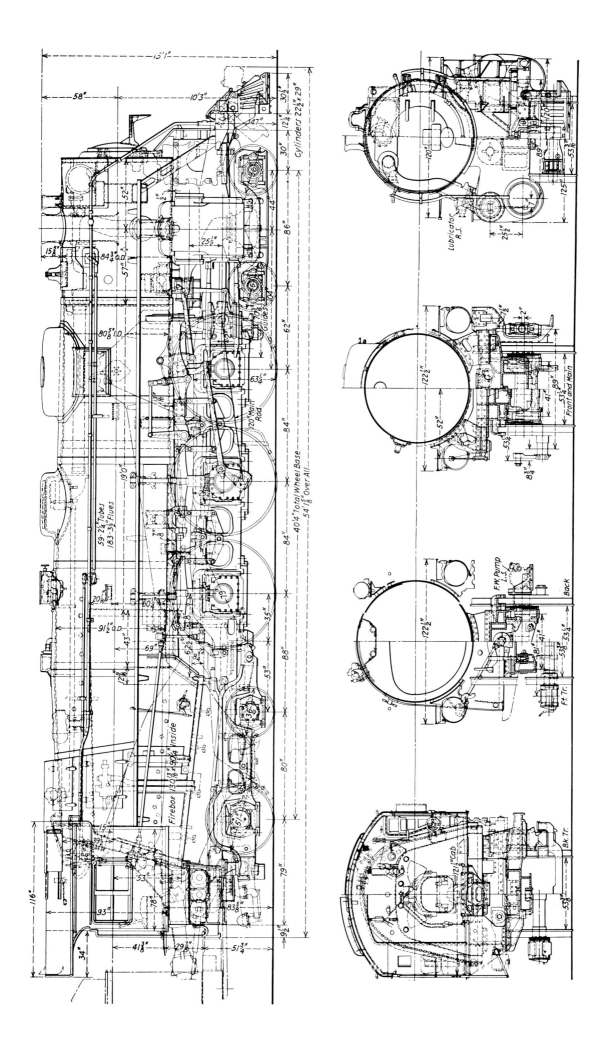

NEW YORK CENTRAL J3a CLASS 4-6-4 HUDSON TYPE LOCOMOTIVE.

ART

Starting on the next page and continuing to the end of this book are the NEW YORK CENTRAL CALENDAR PICTURES from 1922 to 1931 and 1942 to 1947. ALL IN FULL COLOR.

The first six, 1922-1927, pre-date the Hudson-type locomotive but are presented here so we have the full set.

New York Central continued to issue calendars till 1954 with themes being diesels or passenger cars. Costs necessitated our not being able to use them but we would have liked to display the entire series. There were no calendar paintings from 1932 through 1941..

There will be a few blemishes and imperfections in these calendars and posters (in front of book), which are due to imperfect copy and not the fault of the lithographers, Staufer Litho Plate. (my brother's business)

New York Central

NEW YORK CENTRAL 1953 CALENDAR PAINTING BY LESLIE RAGAN.
We like his blocky sculptured style. Things have a third dimension and strength. This same artist painted the Cleveland Terminal poster found on page 11 of this book. His style is the same after twenty three years.

A Painting Entitled: "THE MEETING OF THE WAYS"—By Stanley M. Arthurs.
In the background is the "DeWitt Clinton," the first regular passenger train in America, crossing the Albany Post Road. Its initial trip was made on August 9, 1831, on strap-iron rails, the 17 miles from Albany to Schenectady, over the Mohawk & Hudson Railroad, the original unit of the New York Central system.

= and Today

The New Empire State Express Passing West Point in the Highlands of the Hudson.　1942

The 20th Century Limited speeding through the Heart of Industrial America. 1943

The Century in the Highlands of the Hudson. 1944

The 20th Century Limited on the Historic Water Level Route. 1945

For the Public Service. 1946

Twilight on the Hudson River. 1947